Discover

ELAINE WALKER

TEACHER'S BOOK 3

Longman

Longman Group UK Limited,
Longman House, Burnt Mill, Harlow,
Essex CM20 2JE, England
and Associated Companies throughout the world.

First published 1988
Fourth impression 1990

Set in 10/11 pt Palatino roman
Produced by Longman Singapore Publishers (Pte) Ltd.
Printed in Singapore

ISBN 0-582-51436-3

Acknowledgements
The publishers are very grateful to Steve Elsworth for
his work on the Activity Book and Speechwork
section of this Teacher's Book.

Contents

Introduction

Who the course is for

Discoveries Students' Book 3 is the third in a course for students in secondary education. It is suitable for students who have completed Discoveries Stages 1 and 2, or 180–240 hours of English study. It provides 90–120 hours' work.

Description of the course

The course consists of the following:

1. The Students' Book

This contains fifty lessons. Every fifth lesson is a 'Roundup' lesson which provides a grammatical summary of the previous four lessons and revises the language introduced in those lessons. For reference at the end of the book, there are cues for the recorded oral exercises, a lesson-by-lesson list of words and expressions and a list of common irregular verbs.

2. The Activity Book

This provides extensive further practice of the language introduced in the Students' Book. It can be used for quiet study in class or for homework. Keys and tapescripts are given in the Lesson notes in the Teacher's Book.

3. The recorded materials

There are two sets of recorded materials. Set 1 contains the dialogues and the literary passages from the Students' Book, and the listening exercises from the Students' Book and the Activity Book. Set 2 contains the oral exercises and speechwork exercises.

4. The Teacher's Book

This provides detailed lesson-by-lesson teaching notes with teaching suggestions for each lesson, tapescripts of the recorded material at the appropriate points, and keys to all exercises in the Activity Book. At the end of each set of Lesson notes, there are suggestions for extra activities. At the back of the Teacher's Book, there are three indexes: a grammatical summary, a language use index and an alphabetical word list of active words and expressions with phonetic transcriptions.

Principles behind the course

1. Language use and grammar

After the first two years of learning a new language, students can often feel overwhelmed by the amount of new language still to be learnt. It is important at this stage to ensure that progress continues steadily and that the foundations of the language are securely laid without losing the students'

enthusiasm and will to learn.

Young learners usually find language learning fun if they are actively involved in using the language, whether it be to communicate ideas, solve problems or play games. To keep their attention, a balance has to be found between encouraging the students to use the language creatively and fluently, and consciously practising and studying grammar. At this stage of their learning, they will find that they are already familiar with some of the grammar points being practised. At the same time as learning new grammar, they are revising grammar learnt previously and expanding their understanding of it. It is important to provide students with a cyclical syllabus which constantly recycles the language covered so that the students can learn to use all the language they know. This is what Discoveries Stage 3 aims to do.

To take account of the students' age and level, the approach to grammar in Discoveries Stage 3 is more cognitive than in Discoveries Stages 1 and 2. Students are likely to have a greater awareness of grammar and will want to name structures and analyse them. There is therefore a greater emphasis on grammatical labels and these are used extensively in the grammar summaries.

2. Vocabulary

Discoveries has a rich vocabulary content to give learners plenty of opportunity to learn new words. The course presents 'common core' vocabulary through dialogue, text and exercise material. This is subsequently recycled in the Activity Book in vocabulary exercises, word games and crosswords.

Words and expressions for active learning and use are presented in a lesson-by-lesson list at the back of the Students' Book. A similar list is provided in the Teacher's Book with the teacher's notes for each lesson, and an alphabetical list, with phonetic transcriptions, is provided at the back of the Teacher's Book.

3. The four skills

Speaking

After the presentation of new language, situations for practice are provided to encourage maximum involvement of all the learners, both in controlled and free stages of production. In Discoveries, systematic practice of spoken language occurs in the following pattern:

   a. listen and repeat the new language
   b. controlled pair practice in simple exchanges
   c. oral exercises and speechwork practice
   d. pair or group practice in freer contexts such as communication activities and games.

Listening

The listening skill is developed through tasks based on both scripted and authentic listening material, as well as through dialogue and teacher interaction. Discoveries Students' Book 3 contains a significant amount of authentic listening material, as it is important that students at this stage of learning English develop the skill of listening to natural, ungraded English. The tasks provided guide students' listening and train them to listen for overall gist or specific information rather than to concentrate on every word. Even though the language level of the authentic listening texts may seem to be above the level of the students' speaking and writing skills, the tasks provided do not require students to understand every word, and are appropriate to their current linguistic ability.

Reading

Discoveries emphasises reading as an essential ingredient in the learning process and a key skill in general education and academic progress. Students are introduced to a variety of text types, the tasks for which differ according to the purpose of the text. Students are encouraged to scan for specific information, to read for gist and, through a series of guided steps, to extract and summarise key information.

Discoveries Students' Book 3 makes extensive use of authentic reading material, to take account of students' higher level of English and their greater maturity. At this level, it is important that students start reading English for pleasure. The Students' Book therefore includes seven literary extracts taken from Longman readers and it is hoped that these will encourage students to read further outside the classroom.

Writing

The development of the writing skill is closely linked to the development of reading. Writing is seen as an aid to learning and consolidating new language, as well as a special skill which must be carefully developed as part of a learner's general education. Extended writing tasks are always guided, often related to the learner's experience and linked to reading texts wherever appropriate, thus providing students with a model on which to base their own writing.

General teaching techniques

1. Dialogues and texts

Each lesson opens with a text or dialogue. This may be used as the basis for presentation of grammar or to consolidate a presentation given beforehand. The dialogues and literary texts are also recorded on tape. The other texts are for reading purposes only.

Dialogues

Suggested procedure:
  a. Students look at the picture while you ask questions to establish the situation.
  b. Pre-teach any vocabulary that is essential for students' understanding of the dialogue.
  c. Students read the focus questions in their books or on the board.
  d. Play the tape. Students listen with their books closed or with the dialogue covered up.
  e. Check the answers to the focus questions.
  f. Students read the comprehension exercise.
  g. Students listen again with their books closed or with the dialogue covered up.
  h. Students discuss the answers to the comprehension exercise in pairs.
  i. Check the answers with the class.
  j. Students listen again with their books open. Stop the tape at appropriate points to clarify meaning and check understanding of new vocabulary.
  k. Focus on the examples of the structure in the dialogue for the purposes of presentation or consolidation.
  l. Play the tape again, this time with the paused version for students to listen and repeat. Alternatively, this activity can be done in listening booths or in the language laboratory.
  m. Ask students to read the dialogue aloud in pairs or groups.

Texts

Suggested procedure:
  a. Students look at the picture while you ask questions to establish the situation.
  b. Pre-teach any vocabulary that is essential for students' understanding of the text.
  c. Students read the focus questions in their books or on the board.
  d. Students read silently.
  e. Check the answers to the focus questions.
  f. Students read the comprehension exercise.
  g. Students read silently again.
  h. Students discuss the answers to the comprehension exercise in pairs.
  i. Check the answers with the class.
  j. Focus on any new vocabulary to be taught. Clarify meaning and check understanding.
  k. Focus on the examples of the structure in the text for the purposes of presentation or consolidation.

2. Presentation of grammar

Although the Students' Book lessons begin with a text or dialogue, the teacher's notes sometimes suggest a different presentation of the grammatical structure in focus, in which case, the text or dialogue can then be used to consolidate and practise the structure after presentation.

Suggested procedure for the presentation of grammar:

a. Put the structure into a context, e.g. talking about how someone's life was different in the past, to lead into examples of the *used to* structure.

b. If the students are familiar with the structure, ask questions to try to elicit an example from them, e.g: *Did he drink champagne in the past? Often? Does he now? What can we say? (He used to drink champagne.)* This gives students the opportunity to show their knowledge and involves them in the presentation. If, however, you are unable to elicit an example, quickly provide one yourself.

c. To clarify meaning and check students' understanding, ask concept questions. For example, in Lesson 4 Paul says: *'I've hitch-hiked for three years.'* Possible concept questions might be: *When did he start hitch-hiking? (Three years ago.) And does he (still) hitch-hike now? (Yes.)* Ask these questions at the initial presentation stage and during controlled practice. Try to ask different students each time. The questions can be asked in English or in the L1.

d. Tell students the name of the structure or tense and point out how it is formed, e.g. present perfect simple = *have* + past participle. This can be done in the L1.

e. Highlight any important pronunciation points, e.g. *I have* is usually contracted to *I've*; *for* is usually pronounced /fə/.

f. The students then repeat the model sentence and further example sentences chorally and individually. It is vital that students have the opportunity to repeat new language a number of times to get controlled practice of the form.

g. At this controlled stage of the lesson, any mistakes should be corrected on the spot. Encourage the students to correct their own mistakes.

h. At the end of the presentation, provide a clear record of what the students have learnt. Write on the board example sentences from the presentation with the main stresses clearly marked, the name of the structure, the concept questions and/or a brief explanation of concept (in English or the L1) and how the structure is formed, e.g. *have* + past participle. In the case of tenses, write an example of the positive, negative and question forms and the short answer if all of these have been taught.

The board stage provides a very useful resumé of the lesson and gives you the opportunity to deal with any remaining questions. Try to involve the students in this stage and get examples from them where possible. Tell them not to start copying until the board work has been completed.

i. The students then go on to practise the structure, moving from controlled to semi-controlled to freer practice. The Students' Book provides activities for all the practice stages. In the freer stage of the lesson, the students will need to use the structure in conjunction with other language that they know. At this stage, on-the-spot correction should be minimal. Instead, you can note down mistakes and correct them afterwards.

3. Presentation of vocabulary

Discoveries introduces students to a wide range of vocabulary through dialogues, exercises and listening and reading texts.

Suggested procedure for the presentation of vocabulary which occurs in a text or dialogue:

a. Before you begin to teach, decide which words students need to know in order to understand the text and to do the exercises. Also decide which words to teach for active use and which words should just be explained or translated for passive recognition, i.e. for understanding rather than production.

b. Teach any vocabulary which is vital in order for students to understand the overall meaning of a text or dialogue *before* they read it or listen to it.

c. Get students to read/listen to the text/dialogue. Check their general comprehension of the material before teaching other new vocabulary. Always give students the opportunity to deduce meaning from context. Provide further clarification as necessary.

d. Clarify meaning and check understanding by asking concept questions. For example, in Lesson 12: *Her clothes were strangely old-fashioned. She was wearing a long black dress with a high collar.* Possible concept questions for *old-fashioned* might be: *Do women wear long dresses and high collars today? (No.) Did they wear them in the past? (Yes.) Are (jeans) old-fashioned? (No.) Are (big hats) old-fashioned? (Yes.) What does old-fashioned mean?*

e. Words which are taught for active use should be drilled. Students repeat in chorus and then individually.

f. Encourage students to keep a record of all new vocabulary, preferably in a special vocabulary notebook. Ask them to write the word, the part of speech, the phonetic transcription (if they are familiar with the phonetic alphabet), the main stress marks, an explanation and/or translation and an example of the word in use.

4. Setting up activities

Check students' understanding of the instructions in the Students' Book. In the case of exercises, do the first question or two with the whole class before students start working on their own. In the case of pair or group work activities, elicit the beginning of a model conversation from the class before putting students into pairs or groups. This ensures that all students are clear on what to do before they start. After students have completed a pair or group work activity, set aside time for them to report back to the class or for a few pairs to act out their conversation to the class.

5. Listening activities

Discoveries Stage 3 provides both authentic and scripted conversations. In general, the students should try not to focus on each word but just do the task set. The students do not need to understand every word in order to do the tasks. The following procedures can be used for general guidance:

  a. Set the context of the listening passage and try to stimulate students' interest in it.
  b. Pre-teach any vital vocabulary.
  c. Write focus questions on the board. These should guide students to listen for gist.
  d. Play the tape.
  e. Check through the answers to the focus questions.
  f. Students read the task in their books. Check that they understand it.
  g. Play the tape again, stopping if necessary to give students the opportunity to take notes.
  h. Students discuss the task in pairs.
  i. Check through the task with the class.

This is a general procedure for listening but you may sometimes like to vary your approach or do additional activities. Here are some suggestions.

- Divide the class into two groups. Play one half of the tape to one group while the other group waits outside the classroom. Play the other half of the tape to the second group while the first group waits outside the classroom. Make up pairs with one student from each group. The students summarise the content of the tape in pairs.
- Read the tapescript to the class with one or two changes. Then play the tape and see if they can spot the differences. After students have completed the task, give them the tapescript with some of the words blanked out. Students listen again and fill in the gaps.
- Play the tape in sections. Before playing each section, give the students just two or three questions on that section.
- Play the first few lines of the tape. Give students a few minutes to predict what it will be about. Play the rest of the tape. Students compare their predictions with what they heard on tape.

6. Reading texts

The Students' Book contains two types of reading text: fiction and non-fiction. The non-fiction texts cover a wide range of topics likely to be of interest to students of this age group, and include authentic material such as advertisements and leaflets. The topic-based nature of the texts is intended to provide a stimulus for discussion. The Students' Book generally provides focus questions as well as a task or questions for more detailed comprehension.

The fictional texts are literary extracts taken from a selection of Longman readers. References to the title of the reader, the author and the level are given in the Teacher's Book Background notes. The title and level are also listed at the back of the Students' Book. The extracts have been carefully chosen to awaken students' interest in the stories they are taken from. It is therefore a good idea to tell students where the extract is from so that they can read the whole book. If possible, set up a class library of readers which the students can swap with each other. This will offer students an opportunity to look at different styles of writing.

7. Dictionary skills

As students reach a higher level of English, they need to be trained in self-study skills. A dictionary is probably one of the most useful aids which a language learner can have, but in order to get the most benefit from it, the student needs to know what information the dictionary provides and how to use it properly. The exercises provided in the Students' Book are designed to introduce students to some basic dictionary skills. If possible, all the students should have access to a good monolingual dictionary, e.g. 'Longman Dictionary of Contemporary English' or 'Active Study Dictionary'.

8. Roleplay

Instructions for roleplay are often expressed in cues, e.g. *Say you have been on holiday in France, Say you hope he gets a lift*. Translation of these cues should not be necessary. Make sure students have time to read them before asking them to speak. Elicit the beginning of the roleplay from the whole class before putting students into pairs. This will ensure that students understand what to do. Some students will want to vary or expand what the instructions say. Pairs of students who finish quickly can usefully spend their time writing down a version of their conversation.

9. Writing tasks

Short writing activities like sentence completion can be done in class to vary the pace of the lesson. Longer writing tasks which are set for homework should be prepared in class. Students need time to organise their thoughts, ask for help over suitable words and expressions and ask for guidance in starting the first sentences. The detailed lesson notes give procedures for each writing task as it occurs.

10. Grammar summary

The grammar summary is expressed in a table provided at the end of each Roundup lesson. The summary lists all the grammar introduced in the previous four lessons and should be used as the basis for revision.

Suggested procedure for using the grammar summary:
   a. Give students a few minutes to study the table.
   b. Ask questions to check students' understanding of the concept. Elicit explanations from them where possible.
   c. Ask the students how the structure is formed, e.g: *How do we form the present perfect? (have +* past participle).
   d. Nominate students to make sentences from the boxes.
   e. Give students the opportunity to ask any questions they may have. Use the L1 if necessary.

To vary the procedure, you may like to make use of the following suggestions:
   • Write an outline of the table on the board. Write the headings but not the example sentences. Ask students to copy the table and fill in example sentences. Students check each other's sentences in groups. Go round and make corrections if necessary.
   • Make a copy of the table, cut it up into sections and get the students to piece it back together again.
   • Make a copy of the table and blank out some of the words. Students then fill in the gaps.

11. Oral exercises

Oral exercises can be done every lesson or saved until the end of the Roundup lesson and done in a set. (The latter is most suitable for language laboratories.) The following technique is suggested:
   a. Ask the students to find the appropriate set of oral exercises at the back of their books.
   b. Show how the particular exercise works by playing the examples on the tape while the students follow in their books.
   c. Practise chorally the stress and intonation of the response.
   d. Play the whole exercise and ask students to respond in the pauses chorally and/or individually.
   e. Ask students to go through the exercise in pairs without the tape, using the written cues in their books.

12. Speechwork

Look at the content of the speechwork practice at the end of the Lesson notes for each Roundup lesson, and note the examples. Here is a set of general techniques for using the speechwork:

Pronunciation
   a. Play the tape and ask students to listen and to repeat the two different sounds as presented on tape.
   b. Students then listen to the two sounds together in a sentence on the tape and repeat, e.g: *Hasn't he got nice eyes?*

Stress
   a. Say the stress pattern as it is on the tape, e.g: *dadi dadi.* Exaggerate the stress and beat time with your hand. Students listen and repeat.
   b. Use an example sentence as on the tape to show the stress pattern. Exaggerate the stress and beat time with your hand.
   c. Write the sentence on the board showing the stressed syllables. This can either be written in capital letters or indicated by a box immediately above the stressed syllables or by a stress mark placed before the stressed syllables, e.g:

   THEY were LEAVing.

   □   □
   They were leaving.

   'They were 'leaving.

   d. Students practise this chorally and individually before hearing and repeating the examples on tape.

Intonation
   a. Practise an example from the tape in class, backchaining to make sure the intonation pattern is kept constant, e.g:

   when the alarm rang . . .

   'What were you doing/when the alarm rang?
   b. Give a substitution drill to make sure all the students have grasped the pattern, e.g.
   ss: What were you doing when the alarm rang?
   T: Train came.
   ss: What were you doing when the train came?
   c. Students listen to the examples on the tape and repeat.

Someone I admire.

<table>
<tr><td>**Language use**</td><td>Give personal information
Give information about places
Specify people you admire
Specify things you like and
  dislike</td></tr>
<tr><td>**Grammar**</td><td>Present simple:
Andy Morgan lives in Dover.
He likes playing chess.
Present continuous as future:
*He is taking his 'O' level
  examinations* in two years' time.
Defining relative clauses with
  who:
Andy is an English boy *who lives
  in Dover.*
Non-defining relative clauses
  with *where*:
He goes to Castle Hill Secondary
  School, *where he is in his third
  year.*
Contact relative clauses omitting
  whom and *which*:
Someone *(whom) he admires very
  much* is Bob Geldof. The subjects
  (which) he likes best are
  Geography and Computer
  Studies.</td></tr>
<tr><td>**Vocabulary**</td><td>huge   admire
ambition   cycle
chess   raise (money)
computer important
  studies   spare
examination special
famine relief someone
fashion   in two years'
  design   time
guitar
poetry
politician</td></tr>
</table>

Background notes

'O' level   Ordinary level examinations, which are normally taken at the age of sixteen. The next level is Advanced level ('A' level) taken at eighteen. They are the ordinary and advanced levels of the GCE (General Certificate of Education), replaced in 1988 by the GCSE (General Certificate of Secondary Education).

Princess Anne   The Queen's daughter, now called the Princess Royal. She is president of the charity 'The Save the Children Fund'.

Bob Geldof   A pop star who set up the charity 'Band Aid' and raised millions of pounds for famine relief in Africa.

Meryl Streep   A famous American actress.

Sade   A famous British pop singer.

Winnie Mandela and Bishop Tutu   Well-known anti-apartheid campaigners in South Africa.

Pictures

Students look at the pictures and discuss in groups what they know about the people and what they think of them. Lead this into a class discussion. Use the discussion to introduce the new vocabulary in the text, e.g: *to admire, to raise money, famine relief.*

Text and Exercise 1

Remind the students about Andy Morgan, whom they met in Discoveries Students' Books 1 and 2. The students look at the questions in Exercise 1 and see how many they can already answer. They then read the text. Put the students into pairs to discuss the answers to the questions and to complete the chart. Explain *ambition* and any other unknown vocabulary in the chart.

🔲 Exercise 2

Ask students to draw a chart in their notebooks, like the one in Exercise 1, before they listen. Remind them about Kate and ask them to complete as much of the chart as they can before listening. Play the tape once and give students the opportunity to compare their answers. Play again if necessary.

TAPESCRIPT

Listen to an interview with Andy's twin sister, Kate. Look at your book. Make a chart like the one in Exercise 1 and complete the information about Kate.

INTERVIEWER: Hello, Kate. Can I call you Kate?
KATE: Yes, of course.
INTERVIEWER: Kate, you're Andy Morgan's sister, aren't you?
KATE: That's right. I'm his twin sister.
INTERVIEWER: So you're also fourteen years old.
KATE: Yes.
INTERVIEWER: And do you go to the same school as Andy?
KATE: Yes, we go to Castle Hill Secondary School. We're both in our third year.
INTERVIEWER: And what are your best subjects at school?
KATE: Um, I'm not sure. I think I like Maths and Science best.
INTERVIEWER: When are you taking your 'O' levels?
KATE: Ugh. Don't talk about it! In two years' time. Same as Andy.
INTERVIEWER: And what would you like to be or do when you leave school?
KATE: I don't know yet. I think I'd like to work abroad for a bit, then maybe to go to university.

INTERVIEWER: That sounds sensible to me. And what do you like doing when you're not at school?

KATE: Um, lots of things. I like reading, swimming, dancing. Oh and I'm learning how to rock climb.

INTERVIEWER: That's interesting. Er . . . Now I know this may sound a strange question but is there anyone in the world you admire specially? Someone who's made a big difference to your life?

KATE: Mmm. I can't think . . . Oh yes . . . well, there's my grandmother.

INTERVIEWER: Your grandmother?

KATE: Yes, she's terrific. I admire her a lot. She's had a very hard life. Her husband – my granddad – died not long after they were married and she's had to earn her own living. She's always cheerful and great fun.

INTERVIEWER: She sounds a nice person to know. Thank you, Kate.

KATE: That's OK.

Alternative procedure: Exercises 1 and 2 together

To vary your approach, divide the class into two groups. Give one group the reading to do and the other group the listening. Then pair the students off with one student from each group in a pair. The students ask each other questions to complete their charts. The student who has read about Andy asks questions to complete the chart about Kate and vice versa. When the students have completed the charts, the student who did the reading should do the listening and vice versa so that they can check their answers.

Exercise 3

The students interview each other in pairs using the charts as guidance. If possible, give them the opportunity to talk to a student whom they haven't already worked with in the lesson.

Presentation

Ask the students to look at the text about Andy again and to underline all the examples of relative clauses with *who* and *where*. As the students give you the examples, write the sentences on the board, underlining the relative clauses. Then point out the contact clauses where the relative pronouns are omitted. Write these on the board with the omitted relative pronouns in brackets. The sentences should read as follows:

1. Andy Morgan is a fourteen-year-old English boy <u>who lives in Dover.</u>
2. He goes to school at Castle Hill Secondary School, <u>where he is in his third year.</u>
3. The subjects <u>(which) he likes best at school</u> are Geography and Computer Studies.
4. Someone <u>(whom) he admires very much</u> is Bob Geldof,

5. a man <u>who helped to raise a lot of money for famine relief.</u>

Point out that *who* refers to a person, *which* refers to a thing or an animal and *where* refers to a place. *Where* in Example 2 refers back to *at Castle Hill Secondary School*. Ask the students to look at Examples 3 and 4 and to tell you why they are different to Examples 1 and 5. Point out that:

- in Examples 3 and 4 the relative pronoun is the object of the clause. In Examples 1 and 5 it is the subject
- if the pronoun is the object of the clause it can be omitted
- object relative clauses with no relative pronoun are often called 'contact clauses'
- *whom* is the object relative pronoun for people and *which* is the object relative pronoun for things. *Whom* is not very common in modern spoken English.

Exercise 4

Elicit a few example sentences from the whole class orally first, then ask students to write their own sentences. Get the students to talk about their sentences to each other and to give the reasons why they like/don't like something. A few of the students can then report back to the whole class on their partner's likes and dislikes.

Exercise 5

Start the paragraph off with the whole class and then students can work on their own. Students can use the text on Andy Morgan as a guide.

Exercise 6

Refer students to the paragraph about Andy and their own paragraph about Vicki Wong. Ask them to write a letter to Vicki giving similar information about themselves.

As a possible follow-up, collect the letters which the students have written, jumble them and redistribute them among the students. Then ask individual students to read letters aloud without saying who wrote them. The rest of the class guess who wrote the letters.

Extra activities

1. Talking about photographs

Ask the students to bring in photographs of their holidays to show to each other. Encourage them to point out things/people in the photographs and explain what/who they are, using relative clauses and contact clauses where appropriate, e.g: *That's the Sea View Hotel, where we stayed. That's the family we met. That's the boat we hired. That's South Wood, where my sister got lost.* Demonstrate what to do using your own photographs first.

Activity Book Key

Exercise 1
bread – butter   fish – chips   salt – pepper
milk – sugar   knife – fork   cup – saucer

Exercise 2
see – saw – seen
say – said – said
get – got – got
like – liked – liked
go – went – gone
think – thought – thought
come – came – come
take – took – taken
bring – brought – brought

Exercise 3
good / bad   to lose / to win   friendly / unfriendly
rude / polite   tall / short   upstairs / downstairs
rich/ poor   alive / dead

Exercise 4
IN A CLOTHES SHOP: a scarf, gloves, socks
IN A FOOD SHOP: cheese, vegetables, cream, strawberries
IN A ROCK CONCERT: a singer, a stage
IN A RAILWAY STATION: a ticket office, a platform

I'll carry it.

Language use	Make promises Make offers Refuse offers

Grammar	Modal verb *shall* for offers:
	Shall I take your rucksack for you?
	Modal verb *will/'ll* for offers and
	    promises:
	I'll make some tea.
	I'll send you a postcard.
	Modal verb *needn't* + infinitive
	    without *to:*
	Thanks, but *you needn't bother.*

Vocabulary	journey rucksack term bother need(n't) round You are lucky! a couple of months

Presentation

Try to elicit offers using: *Shall I . . .?* or *I'll . . .* from the students. For example, say: *It's hot in here.* Elicit: *Shall I open the window?* Say: *These books are heavy.* Elicit: *I'll carry them for you.* Provide the appropriate sentence if you can't elicit it. Practise it with the whole class and introduce the positive response: *Thanks, that's very kind of you.*

Dialogue and Exercise 1

To establish the situation, ask the students who they can see in the picture and what is happening. Teach *rucksack.* With books closed, play the tape.

    Students then answer the questions in Exercise 1, individually or in pairs. Play the tape again if necessary. After answering the questions, students can read the dialogue.

    Focus on the offer in the dialogue: *Shall I take your rucksack for you?* and the negative response: *Thanks, Andy, but you needn't bother.* Point out that this means you do not need to take the trouble because it is not necessary. This is a polite way of refusing an offer. *Needn't* is short for *need not* and is followed by the infinitive without *to. Bother* means to take the trouble. Ask students to listen to the paused version of the dialogue and repeat.

Exercise 2

Ask the students to look again at what Cindy says when she leaves: *Bye, everyone! I'll send you a postcard!* Ask them what other things can be said when we leave someone, e.g: *I'll see you on Monday, I'll phone you at the weekend.* Do Number 1 of the exercise with the whole class and then ask the students to do Numbers 2 to 5 on their own or in pairs.

Exercise 3

Practise some offers and responses with the whole class, drilling chorally and individually. Give situations to elicit an offer, then use a gesture or flashcards to indicate a positive or negative response. For example, you say: *You are staying with some friends and their phone is ringing.* S1 says: *Shall I answer it? / I'll answer it.* You show a Yes or No flash card. S2 then responds: *Yes, please. / No thanks, you needn't bother.* Continue with further situations, e.g: *their car is dirty, their dog wants to be taken for a walk, someone is at the door, the washing-up needs to be done.* The students may suggest other similar situations. They then work in pairs on Exercise 3.

Exercise 4

Students write the dialogue on their own or in pairs. They then practise reading it aloud with their partner.

    Oral exercises 1 and 2

Extra activities

1. Planning an event

Put the students into groups of four or five, to plan a party, outing or other event. They must work out what needs to be done and decide who is going to do each task. (If it is possible for students to plan a real event, this would obviously provide very good motivation for the task.) The discussion should incorporate *shall* and *'ll* for offers and promises, e.g: *Shall I make the salad? I'll write the invitations.*

    Each group can then report back to the class. During the reporting back they will need to use the *going to* future or the present continuous as future, e.g: *Anna's going to buy the food. Jack's buying the drinks.*

2. What goes in the rucksack?

Tell the students that they are going to travel round Europe for a couple of months. They can only take a small rucksack. Ask the students to write a list of what they will put in the rucksack and then to compare their lists in pairs and produce one list which they both agree on.

Activity Book Key

Exercise 1
1. Shall I phone her?
2. Shall I make it?
3. Shall I close it?
4. Shall I ask her?
5. Shall I take them (to her)?
6. Shall I tell him?

Exercise 2
1. France   2. Spain   3. Italy   4. Switzerland

I've been to Britain.

Language use	Ask and talk about experiences
Grammar	Present perfect: *Have you ever been* to Britain? *Yes, I have./No, I haven't.* *I've been* to Britain twice. *I've never been* to France. Past simple: *When did you go?* *I went* last summer.
Vocabulary	accident break bone fall off event foreign experience once tonnes (ton) twice tournament

Materials
A map of the world.

Background notes

Wimbledon	The place where Britain's annual international tennis championship takes place. It is called the Wimbledon Championship but is usually referred to just as 'Wimbledon'.
Gabriela Sabatini	A young tennis star from Argentina.
Boris Becker	A young tennis star from West Germany.
Strawberries and cream	The food traditionally eaten at the Wimbledon Championship.

Presentation
The present perfect tense may be revision for the students, as it was introduced in Discoveries Students' Book 2. Start off by briefly contrasting the present perfect and past simple tenses before moving on to student practice. Write on the board: *She's been to Britain once. She went to Britain last year.* Ask questions to clarify the contrast and check students' understanding. Point out that in this case we use the present perfect to talk about something which happened in the past but we do not say when it happened. We use the past simple when we say the time at which something happened in the past, or when the time is understood by the speakers in the conversation. Write the following prompts on the board:

Britain	once	last year
France	twice	three years ago
Greece	three times	in January
Italy	never	in 1986
Spain	often	
Sweden		
Turkey		

You may wish to add to the left-hand list, or substitute the names of areas in the students' country. Ask the students to study the example sentences in the Look! box and to use the prompts on the board to make similar sentences, e.g: *I've never been to Britain.* Then use the prompts to elicit a two- to four-line dialogue. Do one or two dialogues with the whole class, then put the students into pairs.

s1: Have you (ever) been to Italy?
s2: No, I haven't.

s3: Have you (ever) been to France?
s4: Yes, I have.
s3: When did you go there?
s4: (I went) three years ago.

Point out that *ever* means at any time in your life and that *been* is used instead of *gone* in this type of sentence, and is followed by the preposition *to*.

Exercise 1
Point out where Singapore is on the map of the world. Ask the students to look at Vicki Wong's personal experience chart. One half of the class asks the questions, in chorus, and the other half gives Vicki Wong's answers, e.g: *Have you ever been to a foreign country? Yes, I have.* When they have done this, the students ask each other, in pairs, about Vicki, as in the example exchange.

Exercise 2
Think of things that some of your students are likely to have done and write some prompts on the board.

been to the theatre/a big sports event/a rock concert/
   a foreign country
been camping/climbing/sailing
ridden in a helicopter/on a horse
sailed on a ship
seen the President (or Prime Minister)/a film star

Elicit a question from the students by pointing to one of the prompts. Build up a dialogue S-T so that the students have an example to follow, e.g:
s: Have you ever been camping?
T: Yes, I have. I've been camping many times.
s: When did you last go camping?
T: I went camping in Spain in July.
The students then ask and answer in pairs. Refer them to the example exchange in Exercise 2.

Exercise 3
Ask the students to read the extract from Vicki's letter to Andy. With the students' help, write an example paragraph on the board, e.g: *I've been camping many times. I last went camping in July in Spain. It was really great. Have you ever been camping?* Then ask the students to write about one or two experiences from their conversations in Exercise 2.

 Oral exercises 4 and 5

Extra activities

1. Roleplay: Planning an outing

Two friends are planning an outing at the weekend. Ask the class for names of places to visit and ideas for things to do in their town. Write these on the board. In pairs the students decide on two things to do at the weekend. Before starting the roleplay, briefly revise ways of suggesting, e.g: *How/What about . . .?* Point out that *Shall I/we . . .?* can be used to make a suggestion as well as an offer. With the students' help, show how the conversation might begin.

S1: What about going to the Science Museum at the weekend?

S2: Well, I've been there twice before. What about the cathedral? Have you ever been there?

S1: No, I haven't. That's a good idea. Shall we go there on Saturday?

Encourage students to use the language of suggestion and the present perfect for experience.

2. Student talks

Ask students to write notes at home in preparation for a short talk to give to the class about an interesting experience they have had. They can choose what to talk about.

Activity Book Key

 Exercise 1

TAPESCRIPT

Look at your book and listen to the radio programme. Write a tick next to the countries that Cindy has visited, and a cross next to the countries that she hasn't been to.

DISC JOCKEY: It's Saturday, it's ten o'clock, it's the Radio Thames Roadshow. And this is Nigel Rogerson here in Dover. We have a great show for you today. We'll be talking to lots of famous people and we have of course a mystery group for you to discover. It's music, madness, and mystery here in sunny Dover. And first, I'd like to talk to a visitor to our shores. Hi!

CINDY: Hi.

DISC JOCKEY: And your name is . . .

CINDY: Cindy Farrow.

DISC JOCKEY: And you're from the US of A, correct?

CINDY: That's right, how did you guess?

DISC JOCKEY: Gee, I really don't know. But seriously, Cindy, what are you doing over here?

CINDY: I'm travelling round Europe for a few months.

DISC JOCKEY: Great! Where have you been so far?

CINDY: Just the UK, I haven't been anywhere else yet. I'm going to Italy in a week, and then Spain. Maybe France and Germany after that, it depends on the money.

DISC JOCKEY: And have you done much travelling?

CINDY: Yes, I've travelled all over the USA. I've been to Japan, and I stayed a month in Brazil.

DISC JOCKEY: And what's your favourite country? The UK, the USA, Japan, or Brazil?

CINDY: I like them all. They're all very different. It's difficult to compare. Oh, I've been to Argentina, too, I forgot. That's a nice place. I'm really looking forward to Italy and Spain, though . . .

KEY

USA ✔   Brazil ✔   Argentina ✔   UK ✔   France ✕   Spain ✕   Germany ✕   Italy ✕   Japan ✔

Exercise 2

No, I haven't been in a helicopter but I have been in a plane, and it was really exciting. We flew over the south coast of France. Oh, I've driven a racing car, too, at Le Mans but I didn't like that very much. I was frightened!

Exercise 3

Open exercise

Exercise 4

1. Have you ever been to a foreign country?
2. Where did you go?
3. When did you go?
4. Has your sister ever been to Italy?
5. When did she go?
6. Has your father ever been abroad?

Language use	Ask and talk about point and duration of time
Grammar	Present perfect with *since* and *for*: *How long have you hitch-hiked? I've hitch-hiked since I was 16 / for two years.*
Vocabulary	argument dangerous driver friendly lift present allow scruffy attack at once forbid nowadays hitch-hike for murder since rob

Materials
A picture of a teenager.

Read and answer
Ask the students to look at the main picture in their books. Introduce the topic of the lesson and the vocabulary: *to hitch-hike* and *hitch-hiker*. Ask them if they know what the two people in the picture are doing, if they have ever seen anyone hitch-hiking and if they think it is a good idea. Introduce as many of the new words in the text as possible at this stage. The students then read the paragraph and answer the two questions. Check their answers.

Exercise 1
Pre-teach any unknown vocabulary, e.g: *to save money*. Ask the students to read the questions about Danny and then to read his statement. Check through their answers. Students then read Paul's, Susan's and Kerry's statements and answer Questions 2, 3 and 4.

Presentation
Ask the students to read what Paul said again and to tell you when he started hitch-hiking (three years ago). Point out that *I've hitch-hiked for three years* means he started hitch-hiking three years ago and he still hitch-hikes now. Students repeat the sentence. Ask them to tell you when Kerry started hitch-hiking (when she was sixteen). Point out that *I've hitch-hiked since I was sixteen* means she started hitch-hiking when she was sixteen and she still hitch-hikes now. Students repeat the sentence. Explain that *for* is used with a period of time and *since* is used with the point in time when something started. Check that the students understand this difference.

Write up a list of time expressions on the board, e.g:

last year	two years	five minutes
my birthday	1986	two days
three weeks	six months	last year
April	I was twelve	a few years
a long time		

Ask students to write the expressions in a *for* column or a *since* column.

Do a drill where the students have to change the time expression in a sentence and choose *for* or *since* accordingly:

T: She's been in London for two years. Repeat.
S1: She's been in London for two years.
T: 1985.
S2: She's been in London since 1985.

Show the students the picture of a teenager which you have brought to the class and tell them about her/him:

This is Maria, a seventeen-year-old student from Spain. She's studying at an English language school in London. She went to London a year ago as a tourist, and nine months ago she began a course at the language school to improve her English. She lives with an English family. She moved in with the family three months ago because she wanted to practise her English. She studies at the language school during the day. In the evening she goes out with friends or stays at home and watches television or talks to her English family. She likes staying with the English family but sometimes they're busy and can't talk to her.

Ask the students questions about Maria to elicit examples of the present perfect with *for* or *since*, e.g:

T: When did she go to London?
S: A year ago.
T: And is she still there now?
S: Yes.
T: Can you tell me that in one sentence?
S: Maria has been in London for one year.

Go on to elicit the following sentences: *She's been at the language school for nine months / since . . . She's lived with an English family for three months / since . . .* If you prefer, use the story of a real person to practise the structure.

Exercise 2
Do an example S-T before putting students into pairs. Point out that students can use long or short answers, e.g: *I've been at my school for three years* or *For three years.*

Exercise 3
Elicit a few sentences from the students about their families, e.g:

T: Have you got any brothers or sisters?
S: Yes, one sister.
T: What does she do?
S: She's (a student at . . .)

T: How long has she been there?
S: For (two years).
Elicit: *My sister has been (a student at . . .) for (two years)*. Get two or three examples from the class before students write sentences on their own.

▣ Exercise 4

Before students listen for the first time, write a focus question on the board: *Does Jo think hitch-hiking's a good idea?* Play the tape once. Students discuss the answer to the focus question.

Students read the task in their books. Play the tape a second time. Pause two or three times to give the students time to make notes. The students then compare their notes in pairs and ask you any questions they may have on vocabulary. Play the tape again if necessary. As you check through the task with the class, write the arguments for and against hitch-hiking on the board, and keep them there for the next exercise.

TAPESCRIPT
Listen to Jo talking about hitch-hiking. Note the arguments for and against hitch-hiking.

INTERVIEWER: Jo, I understand you do a certain amount of hitch-hiking. Do you think it's a good idea to do hitch-hiking?

JO: Well, there's . . . er . . . good points to it and there's bad points to it but on the whole, yes, I think it is quite a worthwhile method of transport.

INTERVIEWER: What would you say the advantages of hitch-hiking are?

JO: Well the main advantage has to be that it doesn't cost any money at all and I think that's probably the main reason why most people do it. I think it's a very good way of getting to know the country you live in . . . well the country that you happen to be hitching in, because you meet a great variety of people when you do hitch-hike — people from truck drivers to managing directors of firms — it's quite unlikely some of the people who pick you up at times, and also you can develop your art of conversation quite well because you do find yourself in these situations with completely different people, and I think that's another great advantage.

INTERVIEWER: What about the . . . um . . . disadvantages of hitch-hiking?

JO: Yes, well, one thing about hitch-hiking that people don't often emphasise is its unreliability. If you've got to get to a place for a certain time, and it's very important that you do get there for a certain time, hitch-hiking really shouldn't be the method of transport because you . . . you just never know, even if it's a perfect hitching spot, you just might be there for hours, you might be there for minutes. The best situation is if . . . if you're sort of

travelling in an open-ended sense and it doesn't really matter when you get somewhere.

INTERVIEWER: Do you think it's safe to hitch?

JO: Well there is an element of risk in hitch-hiking. I think most hitch-hikers do realise that and there are things you can do to make sure that . . . um . . . you don't find yourself in an unfortunate situation. I mean, er, one thing you can always do is if, when the person turns up with their car, if you don't like the look of them, you can say. 'Well no I'm . . . I'm not . . . I don't happen to be going that way at all.'

Exercise 5

Ask the students to refer back to the reading texts and to the notes on the board to help them with ideas. Ask them what reasons they think the parent gives for forbidding the sixteen-year-old to go on a hitch-hiking holiday and what arguments they think the teenager might use to persuade the parent that it is a good idea. Elicit a model dialogue from the class. Then put students into pairs. Tell them that they may end the conversation as they wish.

MODEL DIALOGUE

TEENAGER: Mum, I'd like to go to England with Sue this summer.

PARENT: But you haven't got any money.

TEENAGER: That's OK. We're going to hitch-hike.

PARENT: I'm sorry, but that's not OK. You can't go on a hitch-hiking holiday.

TEENAGER: Why not?

PARENT: Because it's too dangerous.

TEENAGER: I don't think it's dangerous. And you meet lots of different people. It will be very good for my English.

PARENT: No, I'm sorry, I've told you, it's too risky. And you can't rely on it. You can't go.

TEENAGER: So what am I going to do? I haven't got enough money to travel on trains.

PARENT: You can come on holiday with your father and me.

▣ *Oral exercise 3*

Extra activities

1. Choosing a singer

Tell the students that a famous band/pop group want a new lead singer. They are going to interview people to find one. Half of the class are members of the band and the other half are singers who want to join the band. Give each half of the class time to prepare for the interview. The singers must decide who they are, what experience they have got, why they want to join the band and why they think they would be good. The members of the band must decide what they want to know about the singer, e.g. name and age, the kind of music she/he likes, her/his experience, her/his ability to write music, etc. Then put the students into pairs for the interview.

s1: How long have you been a singer?
s2: For about four years.
s1: And have you sung in a band like this before?
s2: Yes, I'm in a band now.
s1: And when did you join the band?
s2: Two years ago.

At the end, the interviewers can discuss who should be given the job of lead singer. The 'applicants' listen to their discussion.

2. Who will get the lift?
Tell the students that they are driving a car and they see some hitch-hikers asking for a lift. There is a girl on her own, a boy on his own, a boy and a girl together, two girls together and two boys together. Put the students into groups to discuss to whom they will give a lift and why. The groups then report back to the class and compare their decisions. Encourage class discussion.

Activity Book Key

Exercise 1
ACROSS 1. nowadays 5. dangerous 8. murdered
DOWN 2. allowed 3. cheap 4. rob 6. stories
      7. travel

Exercise 2
1. for 2. since 3. for 4. for 5. since

Exercise 3
Open exercise

Exercise 4
FLYING

Vocabulary	hovercraft	by chance
	present	
	get off	
	pass (exam)	
Speechwork	Pronunciation: /d/ admired, /t/ asked, /ɪd/ wanted	
	Stress: da dadi, HITCH-HIKing	
	Intonation: Shall 'I get it?	

Background notes

hovercraft A vehicle which is supported on a cushion of air provided by fans. It is designed to travel over both land and sea.

cops (*pl*) An American colloquial name for the police. Used in the Speechwork section.

Roleplay

Ask questions about the picture to introduce the situation. *What can you see in the picture? What's the difference between a ship and a hovercraft? Where do you think most hovercraft go to from England? Do you know the name of a town in England where you can take a ship or a hovercraft to France?*

Tell the students that Kate is in Dover now and by chance she has just met one of her cousins, Josh. He has got off the hovercraft. Students do the roleplay orally in pairs and then write it.

Listen

Before playing the tape, demonstrate the game to the students. Think of the name of a famous person and get the students to ask you Yes/No questions to find out who the person is. You can only answer *Yes* or *No* and the students can ask a maximum of twenty questions. Play the tape. Stop it twice, after Question 5 and after Question 9, and ask the students to write down who they think it is. At the end of the tape, find out what the students wrote down. The class may continue the game in teams.

TAPESCRIPT

Listen to the radio quiz and see if you can guess the person before the panel.

ANNOUNCER: And now it's time for 'Guess Who? Guess What?' with our quizmaster, Simon Young.

QUIZMASTER: Hello and welcome to Radio Dover's weekly quiz: 'Guess Who? Guess What?' On our panel today we welcome as usual Hilary Archer and David Dean.

HILARY: Hello.

DAVID: Hi.

QUIZMASTER: And our special guests Madeleine Sallis and Robert Cass.

MADELEINE: Hi.

ROBERT: Hello.

QUIZMASTER: Let's start with the first mystery person. Hilary, over to you for Question 1.

HILARY: The name on the card . . . er is the mystery person a he? I mean is he a man?

QUIZMASTER: Yes. One question, nine to go.

DAVID: Is he British?

QUIZMASTER: Yes, he is. Two.

MADELEINE: Is he a TV personality?

QUIZMASTER: No, he isn't. Three.

ROBERT: Is he a politician?

QUIZMASTER: No. Four.

HILARY: Mm. Not a politician. Is it by any chance a member of the royal family?

QUIZMASTER: Yes, it is. Five.

DAVID: Is the person alive?

QUIZMASTER: Yes. Very alive. Six.

MADELEINE: Is he someone people admire?

QUIZMASTER: Yes, . . . er . . . I'm not sure, I think so. Seven.

ROBERT: Did this person go to university?

QUIZMASTER: No, he didn't. Eight.

HILARY: Has this person recently married someone called Sarah Ferguson?

QUIZMASTER: Yes. Nine.

HILARY: Then I think I know. This person is one of Queen Elizabeth's sons.

QUIZMASTER: Yes. I think you've guessed it.

HILARY: It's . . . Prince Andrew.

ALL: Well done!

QUIZMASTER: That makes the score one–nil to the panel. Now for our mystery object . . .

Write

Write the first paragraph of a letter on the board with the students' help. Ask the students to write their own letter in class or for homework.

MODEL ANSWER

(Address)

(Date)

Dear Uncle Harry,

Thank you very much for the chess set. Dad and I play almost every evening and I can beat him now!

I had a busy time at school last year. I played in the school football team and we practised after school every day and played a game every Saturday. We only lost twice! And I was in the school play in March, but I only had a small part.

I've been on holiday for a week now. It's great. I'll come and see you on the first Saturday in August, that's 3rd August.

Love from
Martin

Dictionary skills

Students write the list in alphabetical order. Encourage them to do it quickly. Give them no more than a minute.

Grammar summary

Remind students that:

- the present continuous can be used to talk about the future as well as the present, particularly when a future time phrase is given
- the relative pronoun can be omitted in contact clauses
- the modal verbs *shall/will/'ll* can be used to make promises and offers
- we use the past simple tense when we know the time at which something happened in the past
- we use the present perfect tense
  – when we do not know or are not concerned with the time at which something happened in the past
  – with *for* or *since* to say how long something has happened from the past until now.

Extra activities

1. Jumbled sentences

Write out sentences on cards using the structures covered in Lessons 1–5. Cut each sentence up into individual words. Stick the words of each sentence on the wall in the wrong order, or give them to the students in jumbled order. The students must rearrange them to make correct sentences.

2. Story building

Give the students the beginning of a story: *Last weekend I was on a hovercraft . . .* Then go round the class and ask each student to contribute the next word to build up a story. Go round the class more than once if necessary. Try to keep this game fast-moving. You may prefer to divide the students into smaller groups to play the game.

Activity Book Key

Exercise 1

examination admire scruffy
rucksack forbid foreign

Exercise 2

1. I'll get your suitcase.
2. I'll phone for a taxi.
3. I'll do the washing up.
4. I'll leave a note for your parents
5. I'll give the plants some water.
6. I'll turn off (all) the lights.

Exercise 3

A: How long have you worked here?
B: About three months. Have you worked in a shop before?
A: No, I haven't. This is my first day. What's it like?
B: It's OK. It's like most jobs. Have you met the boss?
A: Yes, she seems nice. How long has she been here?
B: Five or six years. Her parents own the shop.
A: Oh. Have they stopped working here?
B: No, they come in and help when it's busy. Her brother helps, too.
A: I haven't seen him. Has he been in here today?
B: No, not today. It's Friday. He comes in on Saturdays.

Exercise 4

1. a 2. b 3. b 4. a 5. b 6. a

Exercise 5

1. chess 2. cards 3. jigsaw 4. volleyball
5. basketball 6. judo

Exercise 6

1. There are sixteen pieces on each side.
2. You win the game by capturing the other side's king.

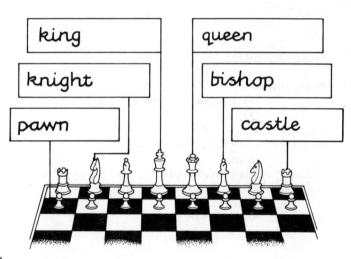

Exercise 7

Open exercise

📼 Speechwork Lessons 1–5

Pronunciation
Listen and repeat.
/d/ /d/ /d/ admired joined allowed

Listen and repeat.
/t/ /t/ /t/ asked walked hitch-hiked

Listen and repeat.
/ɪd/ /ɪd/ /ɪd/ wanted mended hated

Listen and repeat.
I wanted to join the club,
So I hitch-hiked into town,
But I wasn't allowed in.

Stress
Listen and repeat.
da dadi, da dadi, da dadi
HITCH-HIKing, SIGHTSEEing, WINDSURFing

Intonation
Listen and repeat

Shall 'I get it?

Shall 'I phone him?

Shall 'I tell them?

Make offers
GANGSTER: Who's going to get the money?
(Pause)
STUDENT: Shall I get it?
GANGSTER: Who's going to phone Louie?
(Pause)
STUDENT: Shall I phone him?
GANGSTER: Who's going to tell the cops?
(Pause)
STUDENT: Shall I tell them?

LESSON 6 — I've already found a job.

	Language use	Ask and talk about completion of actions
	Grammar	Present perfect with *yet, just, already*: *Has he started* his job? *He hasn't started it yet.* *He's just started it.* *I've already found a job.*
	Vocabulary	album extra company latest (most director recent) hippopotamus part-time magazine already office just petrol station still purse yet staff I'm afraid. ticket inspector That's a shame. You are a pain!

	POSITIVE	NEGATIVE	QUESTION
just	I've just seen Jane.		Have you just seen Jane?
already	I've already done the washing-up. I've done the washing-up already.		Have you done the washing-up already? Have you already done the washing-up?
yet		I haven't done my homework yet.	Have you done your homework yet?

 Dialogue

Ask students to read the introduction to the dialogue. Teach some vocabulary, e.g: *director, company, hippopotamus, staff.* Ask questions to check that students understand the situation, e.g: *Who is Tony Mills? What does his company do? He's going to phone somebody. Why?*

Ask students to close their books. Write these focus questions on the board: *Why does Tony phone Rick? Is Rick going to work for Tony?* Play the tape and check the answers to the focus questions. Explain any more unknown vocabulary, e.g: *part-time job, That's a shame,* etc.

Exercise 1
Students discuss the answers to Exercise 1 in pairs. Play the tape again for them to check their answers.

Presentation
Use examples from the dialogue as the basis for the presentation. Ask students to read the dialogue and underline the examples of the present perfect tense. Clarify the meaning and check understanding: *She's just gone to Europe,* i.e. She went a very short time ago. *I've already found a part-time job,* i.e. some time before now he found a job and so he does not need to find another one. *I haven't started yet,* i.e. up to now he has not started, but he expects to start at some time in the future.

Write example sentences on the board. Clarify whether we can use the adverbs in the positive, negative or question and point out where in the sentence the adverb goes, as follows:

Exercise 2
Refer students to the Look! box. Then practise the question and answer under Picture 1 T–S. In pairs, students then take it in turns to ask the questions under the pictures and to answer them.

Exercise 3
Students read the open dialogue. Check that they understand that *The Cars* is the name of a group, that an *album* is a long-playing record and that *Ghostbusters III* is a film. See if they can deduce the meaning of *You are a pain!* Point out that it is a colloquial expression, only to be used with friends, and that it means the person is very annoying. It is used in a joking manner. Students then study the example sentence in the Look! box. Tell them to use similar sentences in their responses. Start the conversation T–S. The students then do it in pairs. After doing it orally, students can complete it in writing.

Exercise 4
Pre-teach any essential vocabulary, e.g: *ticket inspector, purse.* Students then write the dialogue. Encourage them to think of the ticket inspector's final response. When they have finished, tell them to compare their dialogues in pairs and practise reading them out. Ask one or two pairs to act out their dialogue in front of the class.

 Oral exercises 2 and 3

Extra activities

1. Noughts and crosses
Draw a noughts and crosses table on the board.
Write a verb in the infinitive in each square:

buy	write	do
have	finish	see
start	be	read

Divide the students into two teams. One is the
'noughts' team and one is the 'crosses' team. The
teams take turns to choose a verb from the box and
make a correct sentence with that verb, putting it
into the present perfect, using *just*, *yet*, or *already*,
e.g. *I've just seen Andrew*. If the team produces a
correct sentence, rub out the verb and put in a
nought or a cross. If not, leave the verb in the box.
The winning team is the first team to get a
horizontal, vertical or diagonal line of noughts or
crosses. If students enjoy the game, you can put
them into smaller teams to continue it and provide
them with more 'verb tables'.

2. Anything Is Possible for a day
Tell the students that they have won a competition.
The prize is that they can use the services of the
'Anything Is Possible' company for a day. They
must decide what they would like the company to
do for them.

Activity Book Key

Exercise 1
1. yet   2. just   3. yet   4. just   5. just   6. yet

Exercise 2
1. Sorry. He's just gone out.
2. No, I'm afraid he hasn't finished it yet.
3. Yes, he's already done that.
4. It's the seat. He hasn't got a new one yet.
5. He's already tried that, but it didn't work.
6. You can talk to him now. He's just arrived.

Exercise 3
1. C   2. H   3. K   4. D   5. I   6. F   7. B   8. L
9. G   10. J   11. A   12. E

Take the M20 to Maidstone.

Language use	Ask for and give directions
Grammar	Imperative for directions: *Take the train/M20 motorway to Maidstone.* *Drive down the A20 until you reach the B2163.* *Turn right down/along the B2163.* *Take the next/second turning on the right.*
Vocabulary	motorway enclose route reach signpost turn off tram along turning down How often?

Background notes

M20   M stands for motorway, a very large road with two or three lanes of traffic going in each direction.

A20/B2163   A and B are the classifications given to other roads. An A road is better than a B road. Roads which are not of the required standard are not classified.

tram   (See Exercise 3) a public vehicle, usually driven by electricity, that runs along metal rails ('lines') set in the road.

Presentation

Think of a place near the school which a number of students are likely to have visited. Tell the students that you want to go to this place and ask them how to get there by car and by public transport. Summarise the students' suggestions and use them to produce examples of directions, e.g: *Take the Number 29 bus to . . . and get off at . . . Walk down the street until you reach the traffic lights. Turn right into . . . Road and take the second turning on the left.* Then drill each line. Pay particular attention to the prepositions used. Clarify the meaning of *until*, e.g: *Walk down the street until you reach the traffic lights* means that you continue walking down the street and stop when you reach the traffic lights.

Alternatively, the students can ask you for directions to somewhere and, after giving the answer, you drill each line. When the students have practised the model sentences, give them each a card with a place name on it. Practise the question: *How do I get to . . . ?* and a negative response: *I'm sorry, I don't know.* The students move around the classroom asking each other how to get to the place on their card until they can find an answer to their question.

Letter and 📼 Exercise 1

Students look at the letter quickly and tell you what it is about. Ask them who they think is going to the balloon festival and why. Then ask them to read the letter and complete the telephone conversation in their notebooks. Check the answers with the class. Some variation is possible. Play the tape and ask individual students to say their half of the dialogue in the pauses. Point out the emphatic stress in their last response: *No, turn RIGHT down . . .* The students can then practise the dialogue once more in pairs.

📼 Exercise 2

Pre-teach *junction* and *It's signposted*. Give students a minute to look at the map and ensure they can all find Maidstone. Start playing the tape. Stop the tape after a few lines and ask students where they are on the map to check they have all understood the task. Then continue playing the tape until the end. Play it again if necessary.

TAPESCRIPT

Listen to Rick giving directions to a friend. Look at the map in your book. Follow the route from Maidstone and name the town which Rick is directing Chris to.

CHRIS: So how do I get to this place?
RICK: I'll tell you. Have you got a pen?
CHRIS: Er, yes, I'm ready.
RICK: You're coming from Maidstone, right?
CHRIS: Right.
RICK: So, you take the A229 going north out of Maidstone towards Rochester.
CHRIS: Rochester . . . yes . . . got it.
RICK: When you get to Bluebell Hill, turn right and join the M2 going east.
CHRIS: Hang on . . . M2 going east. OK. Um, how far along the M2 do I go?
RICK: You only go one junction. I think Bluebell Hill is Junction 3 and you get off at Junction 4. Then you follow the signs to Gillingham.
CHRIS: Gillingham.
RICK: I think it's the A278. After a few miles you get to a main road. That's the A2.
CHRIS: Hang on. I didn't get that. You take the A279 off the motorway.
RICK: No, the A278. Anyway it's signposted, as I said, to Gillingham. Then turn right at the A2. Go along the A2 for about a mile and you're there. If you get to Newington you've gone too far.
CHRIS: Right. I think I've got all that. Um, how long do you think it'll take me?
RICK: On your old motorbike? About three days, I imagine!
KEY
Rainham

Exercise 3
Do the exercise orally first. Ask the students how to get to the school from the station and how long it takes. If there is no railway or bus station in the area use the name of a nearby town or place and ask students how to get to the school from there. The students can then write the note to a friend.

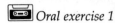 *Oral exercise 1*

Extra activities

1. Where is it?
Students take it in turns to give the rest of the class directions to somewhere from the school, without giving the destination. The student then asks the class: *Where is it?*

2. Strange names
(If this activity is to be done at home, the clues will have to be copied for each student.) Ask students to look at a map of the United States in an atlas and find the following names:
– a place where you can expect to find a lot of sand (Long Beach)
– a lake that you eat your dinner with (Grand Forks)
– a place with the same name as a city in the Midlands region of England (Birmingham)
– a place named after an explorer who discovered America (Columbus)
– a place with the name of a big animal (Buffalo)
– a place where you might find that the sand has an unusual colour (Green Bay)
– a wet city (Salt Lake City)
– a river where all the stones are a strange colour (Yellowstone)
– a white river that you can drink (Milk)

Activity Book Key

Exercise 1
1.

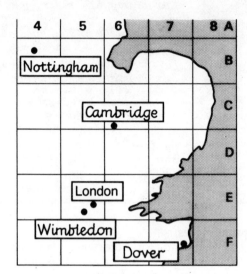

2. Cambridge, Nottingham, Dover, Wimbledon
3. Charing Cross and Waterloo East, Liverpool St, St Pancras
4. Wimbledon, Cambridge, Cambridge
5. Nottingham, Cambridge, Dover, Wimbledon

Exercise 2
Open exercise

Skills	Comprehension, summary and vocabulary skills	
Vocabulary	amazement	bet
	accept	continue
	answer	lose
	begin	reply

Background notes

Literary extract The extract is taken from *Round the World in Eighty Days* by Jules Verne, Longman Structural Readers Stage 3. This is a famous story of a man who bets his friends that he can go round the world in only eighty days.

Read and listen

Write the lesson title on the board. Tell the students that the story is set in 1872 and ask them what they think it will be about. Then write up a few important content words from the passage: *world, three months, eighty days, Phileas Fogg, bet, twenty thousand pounds, this evening, October 2nd, December 21st.* Explain *bet.* Tell the students that *Phileas Fogg* is a name and point out that £20,000 was worth a lot more in 1872 than it is today. Use the words to develop the students' prediction skills. Give them a few minutes in pairs or groups to discuss the content words and guess what this part of the story will be about. Then play the tape and check the students' comprehension by asking them to compare their version with what they heard on the tape. Ask a few students to tell the class, in English, how their version differed from the real text. The students can then open their books, read the text and work on Exercises 1 and 2 alone.

Exercise 3

Point out to the students that the past tenses of the verbs *say* and *answer* appear more than once in the text. After checking the exercise with the class, put the students into groups and give each group a set of cards. The cards should contain all the directly spoken language from the text, with one 'speech' on each card. The verb of speaking, e.g. *they said,* should be omitted.

Ask the students to choose an appropriate speaking verb for each 'speech' and then to put the 'speeches' into the order in which they appeared in the text. The students then read their stories out to each other and see if they agree. Some variations in the choice of speaking verb will be possible.

Joke time!

Do the joke orally with the class first. Take the part of the 'man' and prompt a student into asking *Where to?* Check that the students understand the joke by asking them to translate it and tell it in their own language.

Extra activities

1. Around the world in 80 days

Tell the students that they have eighty days to go round the world. Put them into groups and give each group a map of the world. (If this is not possible, provide one map or globe which all members of the class can consult.) Ask them to plan their ideal trip. They must decide where they are going to go, how they are going to travel, how long they are going to spend in each place and how long it is going to take them to get from one place to another. Their task is to produce an itinerary for the eighty days.

2. Phileas Fogg

Ask the students to make as many English words as possible of three or more letters from the name Phileas Fogg, e.g: *fail, sea, goal.* This could be a competition with a fixed time limit between individuals, pairs or teams.

Activity Book Key

Exercise 1

TAPESCRIPT

Look at your book, and listen to the telephone conversation. Write the details of Sally's travel schedule.

TELEPHONIST:	Harcourt Reeves.
SALLY:	Can I have extension 4583, please?
TELEPHONIST:	Certainly. Trying to connect you.
MARJORIE:	Travel.
SALLY:	Marjorie, it's me, Sally.
MARJORIE:	Oh, hello, Sally.
SALLY:	Can you give me my travel schedule for tomorrow, please?
MARJORIE:	Sure. Ummm . . . have you got a pen?
SALLY:	Yeah.
MARJORIE:	It's a long day tomorrow. Where are you now?
SALLY:	I'm in London.
MARJORIE:	Well, you'll have to hire a car, and drive along the M4 to Bristol. You have to be at Bristol Polytechnic at nine in the morning, and it's the rush hour, so you should leave London at half past six.

SALLY:	Half past six. Oh, dear!
MARJORIE:	There's more bad news to come. You have to be in Liverpool at 1 o'clock.
SALLY:	One o'clock.
MARJORIE:	So you should leave Bristol at 10 o'clock and drive up the M5 and the M6.
SALLY:	M5 and the M6.
MARJORIE:	Then you take the M62 to Liverpool.
SALLY:	Is that the lot?
MARJORIE:	No, I'm afraid not. You have to leave the car in Liverpool and catch the 3.30 train to Manchester.
SALLY:	What?
MARJORIE:	Yes, you have a meeting at Manchester Polytechnic at 4.30.
SALLY:	This is ridiculous! Are you sure you've got the right information?
MARJORIE:	Yes, I'm afraid so. And, er, they want you to come back to London in the evening. There's a plane at eight o'clock from Manchester.
SALLY:	I'm sorry, Marjorie, I can't do that. I think I'd better talk to the Travel Director.

KEY

Destination	Method of transport	Departure time
Bristol	car	6.30 am
Liverpool	car	10.00 am
Manchester	train	3.30 pm
London	plane	8.00 pm

Exercise 2
1. compass   2. penknife   3. torch   4. tie
5. sweater   6. gloves

Exercise 3
1. No, I'm not.   2. No, I haven't.
3. No, she doesn't.   4. No, she isn't.   5. No, I can't.
6. No, they aren't.

Exercise 4
Open exercise

Up, up and away!

Language use	Say what you like Make comparisons Agree and disagree
Grammar	Gerunds (*-ing* form) I enjoy *gliding*. *Gliding* gives me a feeling of freedom. *much* + comparative of adjectives: Gliding is *much more fun than ballooning*. Having a cold is *much worse than feeling sick*. Verb *agree*, present simple: *I agree./I don't agree.*
Vocabulary	basket pilot century sheep crew skating duck wing freedom consist gas burner discover gliding float ground land hang-gliding You can't fool hot-air balloon me! passenger quite honestly

Presentation

Give the students a few minutes to write down all the sports they can think of. Teach any names of sports that students want to know and also any new ones in this lesson: *ballooning, gliding, windsurfing, hang-gliding, skiing, water-skiing*. Ask the students what sports they enjoy to elicit an example sentence: *I enjoy (swimming) and (running)*.

Point out that *enjoy* can be followed by a noun or a gerund (*-ing* form). After a few examples T–S, the students ask each other in pairs or groups.

Work T–S and ask the students which sports they like best. Write on one side of the board the names of the most popular sports in the class. In order to revise the comparatives, ask students why they prefer one sport to another. Write some adjectives on the board to encourage comparison, e.g: *safe, exciting, easy, fun, energetic*. Point out that they can use the gerund as a subject in their reply, e.g: *Windsurfing is more exciting than swimming*.

Show the comparative rules by writing a table on the board (keeping the list of students' favourite sports on the board at the same time). Students copy the table:

One-syllable adjectives:	fast	faster
Two-syllable adjectives ending in *-y*:	healthy	healthier
Most other two-syllable adjectives:	tiring	more tiring
Adjectives of three or more syllables:	dangerous	more dangerous
Irregular:	bad	worse
	good	better

Now ask the students to rank the sports in order for each of the following criteria: cost, healthiness, danger, difficulty, excitement. Ask a few students to tell you what is first and what is last on their lists and why. Use their responses to lead into the presentation of *much*.

T: Do you think windsurfing is more exciting than running?
S: Yes.
T: A lot more?
S: Yes.
T: So, windsurfing is *much* more exciting than running.

Elicit a few more examples from the students and drill them. Point out that *much* is stressed.

Read and answer

With books closed, ask students when the first hot-air balloon took off and who its first passengers were. If they do not know, ask them to guess. The students then open their books and read. Check the answers to the focus questions and deal with any unknown vocabulary, e.g: *like* (as in *like a bird*), *ground, wings*, etc.

Exercise 1

Ask students to read the passage again and discuss the answers to the questions in pairs.

Exercise 2

Ask the students how they think balloons fly. They may use the L1 if necessary. They then read the text to find out. When they have finished reading, ask them to guess from the context the meaning of the unknown vocabulary, e.g: *to float, light, cool* (noun and verb), *to consist*, etc. Find out what they have guessed and clarify the meanings for them. Ask them to tell you, without reading, how balloons fly and then to tell each other in pairs. Students then copy and complete the statements in Exercise 2.

Alison says:

Ask the students to read what Alison said and to tell you why she likes gliding. Point out in particular the sentence: *It's much more fun than flying an aeroplane or a balloon* and ask students to repeat this. Students then read aloud the example sentences in the Look! box.

Exercise 3
Ask the students to make some sentences in pairs
and then to write them in their notebooks. They
should write sentences they agree with.

Exercise 4
Ask the students to look at the example exchange.
Check that they understand and can say: *I agree./
I don't agree. I think it's the opposite.* The students then
read the sentences they wrote in Exercise 3 and
agree or disagree with each other in pairs. They can
go on to produce their own further examples.

 Oral exercises 4 and 5

Extra activities

1. Language activities survey
Write on the board a list of classroom activities, e.g:
*reading, listening to cassettes, writing, working in pairs/
groups, learning grammar, having discussions, playing
games, doing project work,* etc. In pairs or groups,
students ask each other if they enjoy particular
activities or not, and why. Finish off with a class
discussion. You may then wish to contribute to the
discussion and provide reasons why you think the
activities are useful. The discussion should
incorporate the use of *enjoy* + gerund and the
comparative, e.g: *Singing songs is much more fun than
writing.*

2. Word association
The teacher says *hot-air balloon* and asks a student to
think of a word associated with it. The next student
says a word which she/he associates with the
previous one and so on round the class. To provide
an additional activity the teacher can write the
words on the board as the students say them and at
the end of the game the students, in groups, choose
about ten words from the list and make up a short
story around those words. The students read their
stories to each other.

Activity Book Key

Exercise 1
VERBS: land, rise, lift, float
ANIMALS: bird, duck, chicken, sheep
THINGS: balloon, aeroplane, basket, glider

Exercise 2
Open exercise

Exercise 3
Open exercise

Exercise 4
1. in front of 2. behind 3. inside 4. underneath
5. above

Vocabulary	alarm clock	book
	bath	cure
	coalminer	defend
	farmer	dig
	ice skating	draw
	lot	grow
	person	hire
	scientist	persuade
	soldier	produce
	splash	receive
		rule
		sink
		splash
Speechwork	Pronunciation: /l/ lead, /r/ read	
	Stress: da da da, PART-TIME JOB	
	Intonation: 'Take the 'train to	
	Maidstone/and 'get a bus.	

Roleplay

Students look at the picture and tell you what the people are doing. Ask them if they have ever been ice skating and if they enjoyed it. Do the first two lines of the roleplay with the whole class and then put students into pairs. The class can listen to some of the pairs and correct each other's mistakes. Point out that there are some acceptable variations in the language that the students may choose. The students then write the dialogue.

Write

Ask a few students why they like their favourite sport or hobby and ask them to compare it with other sports or hobbies. Remind them of the discussion in Lesson 9, then direct them to the Write exercise. Point out that they should substitute their favourite sport or hobby for ice skating. When they have finished, ask them to read each other's paragraphs and correct any mistakes.

🔲 Listen

Play the tape and ask the students to describe the scenes, using the present continuous tense. Stop the tape after each new sound (there are several sounds within each scene) and ask the students what is happening, e.g: *He is having a bath. He is singing in the bath. He is splashing water.* Students can use the words in their books to help them. Explain any other words that are unknown.

Play the tape a second time, stop after each scene (*not* after each sound) and ask the students what has just happened. If necessary, prompt them into using the present perfect with *just*, e.g: *He has just had a bath.* Point out that it is sometimes possible to make more than one sentence for each scene. After practising the sentences orally, the students write one sentence with *just* for each scene.

TAPESCRIPT
Listen to the four scenes and say what you think has just happened in each case.

1. Someone is singing and splashing water in the bath. Then there is a large heave as the person gets out of the bath.

2. Someone gets into bed, fluffs up some pillows, winds up a clock, turns off a light, sighs and begins to snore gently.

3. Someone drops a vase or glass and breaks it.

4. There is the sound of an owl hooting. A car pulls up. Someone gets out and takes something heavy out of the boot. There is a heaving noise and a splash. The person then goes back to the car and drives away.

MODEL ANSWERS
Scene 1: He has just had a bath.
He has just got out of the bath.
Scene 2: She has just gone to bed.
She has just wound up the alarm clock.
She has just turned off the light.
She has just gone to sleep.
Scene 3: Someone has just dropped/broken a vase/glass.
Scene 4: Someone has just taken a bag/body out of a car and dropped it into the water.
The car has just driven off.

Game

Divide the class into groups. If the number of students in the class cannot be divided into groups of seven, form smaller groups and do not use one or two of the roles. Write the roles on pieces of paper, fold them up and ask each student in the group to pick one out. When all the roles have been allocated, put the presidents together, the farmers together, and so on, and give them a few minutes to prepare their arguments. The students then go back to their original groups and play the game.

Grammar summary

Remind students:
- about the position of the adverbs *yet*, *just* and *already*
- of the prepositions used in giving directions
- that the gerund can be the object or subject of the sentence
- that *much* strengthens the comparative.

Extra activities

1. Project: Sports facilities

The class investigates the sports facilities in the town or area. They compile information on all the facilities available, the cost of membership and/or entrance, the times of opening, details of any classes held and so on. This information may be useful to the class and can be made available to other classes in the school.

2. Guess the sport

Put the students into teams. Each team thinks of a sport or hobby. The other teams ask Yes/No questions to find out what it is. They can only be given the answer *Yes* or *No*, e.g. *Do you run in this sport:* (No.) *Do you do it in the water?* (Yes.) *Swimming?* (No.) *Do you do it in a kind of boat?* (Yes.) *A yacht?* (No.) *A canoe?* (Yes.) *Ah, canoeing.*

Activity Book Key

Exercise 1
1. a   2. b   3. c   4. a   5. a   6. b

Exercise 2
1. I haven't done my homework yet.
2. I've already done the washing up.
3. Miss Harris has just left.
4. I haven't bought anything yet.
5. We've just spoken to your mother.
6. She's already gone to the office.

Exercise 3

do – doing	travel – travelling
work – working	stop – stopping
hit – hitting	play – playing
sit – sitting	watch – watching
pour – pouring	stir – stirring

Exercise 4
Open exercise

Exercise 5
Open exercise

Exercise 6
1. F   2. T   3. F   4. T   5. F   6. T

Exercise 7
Open exercise

Speechwork Lessons 6–10

Pronunciation
Listen and repeat.
/l/ /l/ /l/ lead light long

Listen and repeat.
/r/ /r/ /r/ read write wrong

Listen and repeat.
Is this the right light or the wrong light?
Can't you read? It's the right light.
Oh. Right.

Stress
Listen and repeat.
da da da, da da da, da da da
PART-TIME JOB, FULL-TIME JOB,
YOUTH-CLUB DOOR

Intonation
Listen and repeat.
'Take the 'train to Maidstone/and 'get a bus.
'Take the 'bus to London/and 'get a train.
'Take the 'tube to Heathrow/and 'get a plane.

We were cycling along.

Language use	Ask and talk about continuing actions in the past and completed actions
Grammar	Past continuous + past simple with *when*: *What were you doing?* *We were cycling along when suddenly we saw her.* *She was opening a building when we saw her.*
Vocabulary	building site nearly harbour suddenly old people's somebody home Guess relation who . . . ? wreck Really! cheer What on have a look earth . . . ? inspect

Background notes

old people's home	A home for old people who can no longer look after themselves.
the 'Mary Rose'	A large English warship which sank in 1545. The ship and its contents were preserved intact by thick mud and in 1983 it was brought to the surface and is now in a museum.
Prince Charles	The eldest son of the Queen and the heir to the throne. The future King.
Princess Diana	Prince Charles's wife and the future Queen.
Sarah Ferguson	Wife to Prince Andrew, the Queen's second eldest son. She has the title of the Duchess of York.
Prince Edward	The Queen's youngest son.

Presentation

Tell the students that you have to leave them for a minute to fetch something from the staff room and ask them to keep quiet until you get back. Surprise them by returning to the classroom after a few seconds. Ask a student: *What were you doing when I came back into the classroom?* or *What was (Peter) doing when I came back into the classroom?* Elicit or provide a model sentence, e.g: *(Jane) was talking to (Sarah) when I came back in.* Drill it. Point out in the L1 that the action in the past continuous started before the action in the past simple and that the action in the past simple interrupted the action in the past continuous. Elicit and practise more example sentences about what the students were doing when you came back into the classroom.

Dialogue and Exercise 1

With books closed, pre-teach the unknown vocabulary, e.g: *to guess, to cheer* and *old people's home* (see Background notes). Play the first half of the dialogue up to: *You're nearly right. In fact we saw . . .* Write these questions on the board: *Who did Andy and Kate see? What were Andy and Kate doing when they saw her/him? What was she/he doing?*

The students guess the answers to the questions. Play the rest of the tape and check the answers with the class.

Ask the students how Mr Morgan sounds when he says: *What on earth were you doing?* Point out that *on earth* is used in a question to express surprise. The students then answer the questions in Exercise 1.

Exercise 2

KEY
1. Who was visiting Dover?
2. What was she opening?
3. What were Andy and Kate doing?
4. What were lots of people doing?

Exercise 3

Introduce the exercise by asking the students if they have ever seen anyone famous and, if so, where and when they saw them. Ask the students how many members of the British Royal Family they can name. Pre-teach the vocabulary, e.g: *royal occasions, to inspect, wreck, the 'Mary Rose'* (see Background notes), etc. Students open their books and look at the pictures accompanying the article. Explain that they are photos taken by members of the public whose names are written under each photo. Ask the students who the photos show and what they think each member of the Royal Family was doing at the time. Students read the article and find out.

Ask the students to look at the example exchange in Exercise 3. Divide the class into two groups. One group is *You* and the other group is *Peggy*. Students repeat the dialogue in chorus. Put the students into pairs to roleplay the other three conversations.

Exercise 5

Build up a model dialogue T–S with the help of the class. The students then write their own dialogues and practise reading them out in pairs.

 Oral exercise 1

Extra activities

1. Alibi

Tell students about a crime which was committed at a known time in the past, e.g. the money from the school safe was taken last night after the school had closed. There are two suspected people and the class must interview them separately to find out if they are telling the truth. Send two students out of the classroom to prepare for the interview. Tell them that they must tell the police that they were together on the night of the crime and so they must agree on the story they are going to give.

Meanwhile, the rest of the class, who will play the police, prepare the questions. Each suspect is then interviewed on her/his own. The interview may begin something like this:

A: What were you doing on the night of the robbery?
B: I was having dinner in a restaurant.
A: Who were you with?
B: My friend Alan.
A: What did you eat in the restaurant?

If the suspects give the same answers to the questions, they are not guilty, but if there are differences in their answers they are guilty. If you have a large class, the students could be divided into groups for the game.

2. Project book
Ask the students to find a picture of a famous person they have seen. They put this picture in their project books and write a paragraph about the occasion when they saw the person.

Activity Book Key

Exercise 1
1. I was reading a book.
2. You were watching television.
3. Marie was sleeping.
4. Peter was brushing/cleaning his teeth.
5. We were washing up/doing the washing up.
6. The twins were playing chess.

Exercise 2
1. I was having a bath when the phone rang.
2. We were watching television when Peter arrived.
3. They were playing in the garden when they saw the balloon.
4. You were walking very quickly when I saw you.
5. She was mending her bike when Mr Harris came in.
6. James was going to a disco when I met him.

Exercise 3
Open exercise

Was I dreaming?

Language use	Give background events
Grammar	Past continuous with *while* and *as* + past simple: *As I was walking* through the rose garden, *I saw* a young woman. *While I was walking* along, *I saw* someone in the rose garden.
Vocabulary	adventure dream autumn following clothes strangely collar as old-fashioned while rose stone seat

Background notes

Hampton Court An old palace with large gardens, near London. It was once owned by King Henry VIII, who had six wives. Henry built a great hall, decorated with the arms (emblem/insignia) of Ann Boleyn (c.1507–1536), his second wife, but before it was completed she was executed.

Hallowe'en (AB) The night of 31st October when, according to superstition, witches and ghosts are out. People often have parties on 31st October and dress up as witches or ghosts.

Text

Ask the students to look at the picture. Ask them a few questions about it, e.g: *What is the picture of? What can you tell me about the woman? What sort of clothes is she wearing? Why do you think she's unhappy?*

Pre-teach the unknown vocabulary, e.g: *Hampton Court* (see Background notes), *dark*, *stone seat*, etc. Ask the students to read the passage and to discuss in pairs who they think the woman was. Then discuss the question briefly with the whole class.

Exercise 1

Do this exercise orally with the whole class and point out the emphatic stress used when we correct statements. Students then practise it together in pairs, e.g:

s1: The writer was walking in the park.
s2: No, he wasn't. He was walking in the GARdens at Hampton COURT.

Presentation

Focus on the example of the structure in the Look! box. Give the students practice in making similar sentences using *as* or *while*. Show the students prompt cards to elicit sentences and drill them, e.g:

walk home	meet cousin

While/As I was walking home, I met my cousin.

do homework	have idea

While/As I was doing my homework, I had an idea.

mother phone	cook dinner

My mother phoned while/as I was cooking the dinner.

drive to work	see accident

While/As I was driving to work, I saw an accident.

dog bite me	lie on beach

A dog bit me while/as I was lying on the beach.

Point out in the L1 that:
- the event in the past simple tense 'interrupts' the event in the past continuous
- *while* and *as* mean *during the time that* . . .
- the order of the sentence can be reversed, e.g: *I found a book about King Henry VIII while I was looking at some history books in the library.*
- we normally use a comma after the clause beginning with *As* or *While* when it comes first in the sentence
- the past continuous can be used to describe the background to a story, e.g. what someone was doing, how she/he was feeling, what the weather was like, etc, before the events of a story are given in the past simple.

Exercise 3

Remind the students that the past continuous is used to describe what was going on in the background and the past simple is used to say what happened, i.e. to describe the events. Go through the story outline with the students and ask them which tense should be used for each sentence. Do the first few sentences with the whole class. Students can then work on their own or in pairs. Follow up this exercise by writing some sentences on the board in jumbled order, some describing the background and some describing events, and ask the students to put them into the correct order.

Exercise 4

Before students listen to the tape, give them a simplified oral summary of the story. As you do so, introduce any key words that students need to understand, e.g: *mental hospital, ward, corridor, to lock, figure, broom, patient, no longer, ghost.* Students look at the task for Exercise 4, listen to the story and take notes. Stop the tape once or twice to give students time to do this. They then compare their notes in pairs. Check through the answers with the whole class. Ask the students if they think Evelyn really saw a ghost and encourage some discussion.

TAPESCRIPT
Listen to Evelyn telling a frightening story. Look at your book and take notes.

INTERVIEWER: Evelyn, you're going to tell us a strange story. When and where did it happen?
EVELYN: It happened . . . oh . . . er . . . many years ago, now, in Manchester, which is in the North of England.
INTERVIEWER: What were you doing there at the time?
EVELYN: Well, I was working in a mental hospital to earn some money; and at night you had to go from the ward where you were working and take the keys back to the office; and to get to the office you had to walk along a lot of corridors; and you had to be very careful to lock every door behind you.
INTERVIEWER: So you were on your way back to the office with the keys. What happened?
EVELYN: I opened one door and there was a very . . . er . . . long corridor with another door at the end of it, and windows on the side. As I came through the door, I saw a figure at the other end of the corridor. I locked the door behind me and looked again. It was a . . . a lady . . . um . . . oh . . . maybe sixty, seventy with grey hair. She was leaning on a broom and she was wearing an apron with flower patterns. You see I can remember in great detail even now what she looked like. I wasn't frightened. I thought it was a patient and for some reason she'd got locked in the corridor and was just standing there. I didn't want to frighten her so I didn't call out. I just walked slowly towards her.
Now I can't explain this bit very clearly but when I got to the end of the corridor, suddenly she was no longer there; and I looked all back along the corridor thinking she'd moved but there was just me in the corridor. It wasn't frightening but I do believe in ghosts now and I still know what that lady looks like even years afterwards.

Exercise 5
Refer students back to the story outline in Exercise 3 and ask them to follow the same outline for their stories. Point out again that the past continuous tense is used when giving the background description and the past simple is used to describe the events. Ask a few students to read out their stories when they have finished.

 Oral exercises 2 and 3

Extra activities

1. Finish the story
Give the students the beginning of a ghost story and then put them into groups to finish it as they wish. The groups then read their stories out to each other. The story begins: *It was a dark, cold night and it was raining hard. Helen was walking along a country road. She was walking very fast because she was frightened. Suddenly . . .*

2. Henry VIII and his six wives
Ask the students to find out who Henry VIII's six wives were, and how and why they died, and to write their findings in their project books.

Activity Book Key

Exercise 1
1. collar   2. rose   3. dress   4. stone   5. to cry
6. library

Exercise 2
One evening last year I was working late at the office. It was winter, and it was snowing outside. I was reading some reports when I heard a noise. I looked out of the window but I couldn't see anything. I went back to the reports but as I was working, I had a strange feeling. I felt that someone was watching me through the window. 'This is silly,' I thought. 'The office is on the second floor. It's impossible for anyone to be outside.'
I turned round to pick up a book and saw something in the mirror. It was a face and it was watching me through the window. When I turned back, the face wasn't in the window any more – but it was still in the mirror. It stayed there all night, watching me as I worked. The next day, I looked at the ground outside the building. There were no marks in the snow underneath the window. It was clean and fresh. There were no marks on the window itself and nothing in the mirror. But I know I saw a face. And there's something else. That night was 31st October, or Hallowe'en, the night when ghosts call and witches walk. Since that night, I have believed in ghosts.

Exercise 3
1. I said: "The gardens are closing now."
2. She said: "This is silly."
3. The ticket inspector said: "Tickets please."
4. The old woman said: "Where's your mother?"
5. "I can't find my little brother," she said.
6. She said: "Could you tell me the time, please?"

Language use	Comprehension, summary and vocabulary skills	
Vocabulary	citizen	cover
	drop	cry
	jewel	fly
	ruby	pour
	sapphire	rub down
	statue	miserable
	swallow	
	sword	
	tears	

Background notes

Literary extract
The extract is taken from *The Happy Prince*, a story by Oscar Wilde contained in *The Young King and Other Stories*, Longman New Method Supplementary Readers Stage 3.

Morden Manor (AB)
A manor is a large old house with land. In the past, the manor was the house which the local lord lived in.

Read and listen

To introduce the subject of the reading passage and pre-teach some of the vocabulary, ask the students questions about the picture, e.g: *Who's the person in the picture? Is he real? What's he made of?*

Ask students to describe the prince and, making use of their responses, teach key vocabulary *statue, gold, jewels, sapphires, sword, ruby, to cry, a tear, cheek, swallow*. Ask students why they think he is called the Happy Prince and why he is crying. Listen to some of their ideas, then play the tape for students to find out the answers.

Ask students to read the story and to guess the meaning of the following words: *covered* (line 3), *citizens* (line 6), *rest* (line 11), *wing* (line 12), *drop of water* (line 12). They can work alone or in pairs. Listen to their suggestions and clarify the meaning of the vocabulary as necessary.
Point out that:

• *Once upon a time . . .* is a traditional way of beginning stories and means: One day some time in the past . . .
• *Just as* + past continuous (line 11) means at the exact moment he started doing something
• *He saw tears running down the prince's golden cheeks.* (line 14) means: He saw tears. They were running down the prince's golden cheeks.

Give the students some practice in using the present participle, as in the example in line 14. Write some pairs of sentences on the board and get the students to make them into one sentence, e.g. *I saw the Prime Minister. She was getting into a car. = I saw the Prime Minister getting into a car.*

Encourage some discussion of the story. Explain that this is only part of the story. Ask the students to predict what might happen and how the swallow might help the prince. (In the story, the prince asks the swallow to pick out the jewels from his eyes and sword and take them to the poor people who are suffering in his kingdom. In the end, the prince has no jewels or gold covering him at all.) Suggest that the students read the whole story if they are interested in it.

Exercise 1

Ask students to read the story again and write the questions. Then get them to ask and answer the questions in pairs. Check them with the whole class.

KEY
1. A: Why was the statue beautiful?
   B: Because it was covered in gold and jewels.
2. A: Where was the ruby?
   B: On his sword.
3. A: Where was the swallow going?
   B: To Egypt.
4. A: Why did the swallow stop?
   B: To take a rest.
5. A: Where did the swallow stop?
   B: At the statue's feet.
6. A: What fell on him?
   B: A large drop of water.
7. A: Why was the Happy Prince crying?
   B: Because he could see how many people were poor and miserable.

Exercise 2

Check the students' understanding of the words in the box. The students then copy and complete the sentences in their notebooks.

Exercise 3

Ask the students to write a rough summary of the story with their books closed. Then ask a few students to read out their summaries. Make corrections as necessary. Use these summaries as the basis for eliciting from students what they should include in a summary. Elicit or point out that a summary tells us about the main events in a story but does not include any of the background information. The students then write the summary for Exercise 3. They may refer back to the story if necessary.

KEY

Opening
Once upon a time high above a city stood the beautiful statue of the Happy Prince.
Event 1
One night a swallow flew over the city.
Event 2
He stopped to take a rest at the statue's feet.
Event 3
A large drop of water fell on him.
Event 4
He looked up and saw tears running down the prince's golden cheeks.

Extra activities

1. Local statues
Ask the students to find out the history of any local statues. They may wish to buy a postcard of a statue, write about its history and put this in their project books.

2. Vocabulary check
Write on the board the new vocabulary dealt with in this lesson, e.g: *statue, covered*, etc. Ask the students to translate each word. They should then compare their translations in pairs or in groups and help each other where necessary. They should check any unknown or disputed words in a dictionary.

Activity Book Key

Exercise 1
1. Major Morden died at 9 pm.
2. He was walking in his garden (with his dog).
3. The police are talking to the people who were in the house (at the time).
4. There were four people in the house.
5. Because the walls of the manor were too high for anybody to climb over.

 Exercise 2

TAPESCRIPT
Look at your book. Listen to the police interviews. Take notes and decide who killed Major Morden.

INSPECTOR MILLER:	Now, you're Peter Morden, aren't you, Major Morden's second son?
PETER:	That's right.
INSPECTOR MILLER:	Where were you at nine o'clock last night?
PETER:	I was in bed, asleep. At nine o'clock I heard Buster barking . . .
INSPECTOR MILLER:	That's the major's dog?
PETER:	That's right. Well, the dog was making a terrible noise, and it woke me up. So I opened the bedroom window and looked out. Then I saw my father, lying on the ground under my window, about ten metres below me. But I didn't see anything else.

INSPECTOR MILLER:	Mm.
PETER:	How did he die, Inspector?
INSPECTOR MILLER:	He was hit on the head by something – but we don't know what.
INSPECTOR MILLER:	Susan, you work in the kitchen, don't you?
SUSAN:	That's right, sir.
INSPECTOR MILLER:	What were you doing at nine o'clock last night?
SUSAN:	I was cleaning the kitchen floor, sir.
INSPECTOR MILLER:	Did you see anything?
SUSAN:	No, sir, I didn't see the major at all last night.
INSPECTOR MILLER:	Did you see anybody?
SUSAN:	No, sir, nobody at all, except Peter.
INSPECTOR MILLER:	What was he doing?
SUSAN:	He came to the kitchen to get a block of ice. He uses ice for his chemistry experiments, so we keep big blocks of it in the freezer.
INSPECTOR MILLER:	What time was this?
SUSAN:	About nine o'clock, sir.
INSPECTOR MILLER:	You're Patrick Lessing?
PATRICK:	That's right. I work in the gardens. I was working in the garden last night when the major was killed.
INSPECTOR MILLER:	What did you see, Mr Lessing?
PATRICK:	Well, I saw two very strange things. The first one was Lady Morden, the major's wife . . .
INSPECTOR MILLER:	Yes, yes, I know who Lady Morden is.
PATRICK:	Well, she was standing on the grass, looking at the house. She was staring at it very hard, looking at something. I don't know what . . .
INSPECTOR MILLER:	And then?
PATRICK:	And then, five minutes later, Peter ran past. He was carrying something . . .
INSPECTOR MILLER:	What was it?
PATRICK:	I don't know. It looked like a big block of ice. Anyway, he ran up to the garden wall and he threw it over the wall. Then he ran back to the house.
INSPECTOR MILLER:	Thank you, Mr Lessing. That's very helpful.
INSPECTOR MILLER:	Lady Morden, I'm afraid I have to ask you some questions about your husband . . .
LADY MORDEN:	Yes, I understand.
INSPECTOR MILLER:	Were you in the garden last night?
LADY MORDEN:	Yes, I was.
INSPECTOR MILLER:	And what did you see?
LADY MORDEN:	Well, I was looking towards the house and I thought I saw something fall out of Peter's window.
INSPECTOR MILLER:	What did it look like?

LADY MORDEN:	Well, I didn't see it very clearly. It looked large and white, but I couldn't really see it properly. Then I heard the dog, and I walked to the house. My husband was lying on the ground, and the dog was making a noise, but there was nothing else there.
INSPECTOR MILLER:	How long did it take you to get to the house?
LADY MORDEN:	About three or four minutes, I don't walk very quickly.
INSPECTOR MILLER:	Was there anyone else by your husband when you got to the house?
LADY MORDEN:	No, nobody at all, I was the first person to get there.
INSPECTOR MILLER:	I think you're wrong, Lady Morden – and I think I know who killed your husband, too.

KEY

Peter Morden killed the major. He dropped a block of ice on the major's head, then ran downstairs, picked up the ice, and threw it over the garden wall.

Exercise 3
1. lift   2. rose   3. bet   4. passenger
5. wonderful   6. chicken

Exercise 4
All five words are verbs and nouns. Answers will vary according to the dictionaries used.

Language use	Ask for information about the past
	Describe how things affect the senses
Grammar	Stative verbs *look, feel, sound, smell, taste:*
	It looks nice/great/good.
	That sounds exciting/wonderful.
Vocabulary	actress behead
	agent look
	eyebrows smell
	hairstyle sound
	part (in film) taste
	pudding confident
	role delicious
	sense of leading
	humour on location

Materials
A picture of a beautiful holiday resort.
Something to eat.

Background notes
The Tower of London	Parts of the building date from 1087. In its time, it has been used as a fortress, a palace and a prison. It was most famous as a prison and many famous people were executed there. It is now a museum. The Crown Jewels are kept there.

Presentation
Show the students a picture of a holiday resort. It should be somewhere that looks beautiful. Choose a place that the students are not likely to be familiar with. Tell the students that this is where you are thinking of going for your next holiday. Ask for their reactions. Elicit or provide a model sentence with *look*, e.g: *It looks beautiful.* Students repeat the sentence chorally.

Explain that it is a nice place. Give students some information about it, e.g: *The sea is very warm, the beach is always quiet, there are some very good restaurants in the town, the people are friendly.* Point out that you have not been there yourself but this is what you have heard from the travel agent. Elicit or provide a model sentence with *sound*, e.g: *It sounds nice.* Students repeat.

To introduce the next three verbs, bring into the classroom something that the students can smell, taste and feel, e.g. something to eat. The students can then touch it with their eyes closed: *It feels horrible*, smell it: *It smells awful/nice*, and taste it: *It tastes horrible/delicious.*

Direct students to the Look! box in their books. Check their understanding of the adjectives and teach any that are new. Point out to the students that these verbs are most frequently used in the present simple tense, as in the examples, and that they cannot be put into the continuous form in this context.

Read and answer
Ask the students if they like the cinema and if they have seen any good films recently. Teach a set of vocabulary on the theme of films, including those items which appear in the text, e.g: *director, producer, agent, actor, actress, to act, to play a role, the leading role, a film, to film, on location*, etc.

Ask the students to look at the questions and then to read the article. Check their answers to the questions. Clarify the meaning of any other unknown vocabulary, after encouraging students to deduce the meaning from context. (N.B. *5'2"* = five feet two inches = approximately 1 metre 50 cm.)

Ask the students to find examples of the stative verbs (*look/feel* etc.) in the article.

Exercise 1
Point out to students that it is not necessary to write full sentences when completing the file.

Exercises 2 and 3
Ask the students to refer to the article to find the answers to the questions in the roleplay. Students do the roleplay in pairs. Some students may give longer answers than others and offer more information to the interviewer. Some variation in the responses is possible.

Exercise 5
Point out that this is an exchange. A says: *Come in! I'm baking some bread!* and B says: *It smells delicious!* Read the remarks and elicit an appropriate response from the students. The students then do the exercise again in pairs.

 Oral exercise 4

Extra activities

1. Expressing your reactions
Ask the students to bring in things for each other to look at, hear, feel, smell and taste. Ask each student to bring in at least one thing. The students then move round the classroom telling each other about what they have brought and responding, e.g:
s1: This is my new perfume/soap.
s2: Mm. It smells lovely./Ugh. It smells awful.

2. Project book

Ask the students to find a picture from a film they have seen and to stick it in their project books. They then write a description of the film and what they thought of it.

Activity Book Key

Exercise 1
1. F   2. E   3. B   4. A   5. C   6. D

Exercise 2
1. He saw someone leaving the house.
2. He saw someone going into the house.
3. He saw someone cleaning the windows.
4. He saw someone watching the street.
5. He saw someone getting into a car.
6. He saw someone watching him.

Exercise 3

self-confident ✔	bossy ✗
scruffy ✗	lively ✔
good-tempered ✔	fierce ✗
moody ✗	greedy ✗
helpful ✔	unhealthy ✗

Exercise 4
Open exercise

Vocabulary	forest	pull
	police officer	world-famous
	robber	tightly
Speechwork	Pronunciation: /s/ ice, /z/ eyes	
	Stress: dadi dadi,	
	I was WORKing	
	Intonation: 'What were you	
	doing/when the alarm rang?	

Background notes

The Crown Jewels The crowns, jewels, etc, worn by the Queen or King on special occasions. The collection is kept in the Tower of London.

Covent Garden (See Listen exercise.) A fashionable area in central London with a lot of shops, restaurants and cafés, and an indoor and outdoor market.

Roleplay

Ask the students if any of them have ever seen a robbery. If so, ask them to tell the class about it. Elicit the type of questions a police officer may ask a witness to a robbery, e.g: *Where were you? What did you see? What were the robbers doing? What were you doing when you saw the robbery?*

Students open their books and look at the pictures of the robbery. Ask them to tell you what happened.

The students look at the instructions for the roleplay. Elicit the first four lines of the roleplay from the whole class before putting students into pairs. Remind the students of the *see + -ing* structure practised in Lesson 13. Ask them to make the following two sentences into one sentence: *I saw two robbers. They were stealing the Crown Jewels.* = *I saw two robbers stealing the Crown Jewels.*

When the students have completed the roleplay, ask a few of the pairs to act out the dialogue in front of the class and correct mistakes where necessary. A number of variations are possible. The students then write the dialogue.

MODEL ANSWER
POLICE OFFICER: What's your name?
YOU: I'm Steve Brown and I'm a student.
POLICE OFFICER: What did you see?
YOU: I saw two robbers stealing the Crown Jewels.
POLICE OFFICER: What were they wearing?

YOU: One was wearing a striped T-shirt and jeans and the other was wearing an open-necked shirt, jacket and jeans.
POLICE OFFICER: What were they carrying?
YOU: The Crown Jewels.
POLICE OFFICER: Were there any other people with them?
YOU: There was a woman waiting for them in a car and they drove away together.

Listen

Write a focus question on the board: *Who did Jane see?* Play the tape once for students to answer the question. Play the tape again. Students complete the information in the chart. Check the students' answers with the whole class and then ask them to write out another chart and complete it with information about a famous person they once saw. The information they give can be real or imaginary. The students then ask each other about their experiences.

TAPESCRIPT
Listen to Jane talking about a famous person she once saw. Look at your book and complete the information in the chart.

INTERVIEWER: There must be a lot of famous people wandering around London but you don't often get to see them, do you? Have you ever seen anybody famous, Jane?
JANE: Not very often, no, but quite recently I did see somebody very famous indeed. In fact it was on the 21st April 1986.
INTERVIEWER: And what were you doing at the time?
JANE: Well, I was in Covent Garden, which is in central London, having a meal with a friend of mine one evening; and we were in the restaurant eating our meal and enjoying ourselves and we noticed that there were a lot of people outside in the street and we wondered what was going on. So I asked somebody sitting at the next table: 'What's going on?' and this person said: 'Well the Queen's coming. It's the Queen. She's coming to Covent Garden.' Well I was very excited 'cos I'd never seen the Queen and I thought: 'Oh, I must go and see the Queen.' So we went out of the restaurant and the street was crowded with people. There were hundreds of people there, and we pushed our way to the front and at the front there were about twenty or thirty small children, and they were standing there, and they'd got flowers in their hands and they were waiting to give these flowers to the Queen when she arrived. And a couple of minutes later, she did arrive. The car came round the corner and stopped and the Queen stepped out and she was smiling, and she looked so happy; and the crowd immediately started singing 'Happy Birthday' because it was the Queen's sixtieth birthday.

Writing

Ask the students to read the outline of the story. Help them with vocabulary. Ask the students what tense we normally use to describe events in the past and what tense we use to describe general background details. Point out that we do not use the past continuous if the details we are describing are always true, e.g: *The house stood next to a school,* or when we are using a stative verb, e.g: *The forest smelt lovely.*

Ask the class for suggestions on how they might describe the forest and the weather. Write some suggestions on the board, e.g:

Describe the forest
The trees were very thick and tall.
It was dark inside the forest.
The birds were singing.
I could hear animals walking through the forest.

Ask the students to complete the story and to write it in full in their notebooks. The students can then pass their notebooks around and read each other's stories.

Dictionary skills

After completing the task, ask the students to look up any words they do not remember the meaning of.

Grammar summary

Remind the students that:
- the past continuous can be used to give general background details and the past simple to describe events
- the past continuous is often 'interrupted' by an event in the past simple
- *as* and *while* generally precede a clause in the past continuous
- *as* and *while* mean *during the time that . . .*
- stative verbs do not generally take the continuous form.

Extra activities

1. Consequences

Write on the board: 1. *Where were you? Describe the place.* 2. *Describe the weather.* 3. *Who were you with?* 4. *What happened?* 5. *What did your 'friend' do?* 6. *What did you do?* 7. *What happened in the end?*

Give the students a few minutes to think of a story answering the seven questions. Tell them the story does not need to be serious. Put the students into groups of six or seven. Give each student a piece of paper. Ask them to write their answer to Question 1 at the top and then fold over the paper so that the answer cannot be seen. Each student passes the folded paper to the student on their right

and writes the answer to Question 2 on their new piece of paper. They fold it over and pass it on again, and so on.

When all the students have answered all the questions, ask them to read out the 'stories' to their group. The mixture of answers from different students' stories should create some amusement. Each group can then choose their best story to read to the rest of the class.

2. Interview a witness

Ask the students to find a newspaper report about a robbery or other crime and bring it into class. The students imagine that they saw the crime take place and, in pairs, they roleplay an interview between a police officer and a witness to the crime. The students can then write the witness's account.

Activity Book Key

Exercise 1
1. No. When I saw James, he was crying.
2. No. When I saw Marie, she was feeling awful.
3. No. When I left, they were baking bread.
4. No. When I met Pete, I was working in a restaurant.
5. No. When I saw you, you were talking to a girl.
6. No. When the boss came back, we were having lunch.

Exercise 2
I was walking home from school one day when I saw a girl that I knew. She was sitting on a stone seat, looking at something, but I couldn't see what it was. So I walked over to her and said: 'Hello. What's that?' She jumped. 'Oh!' she said, 'You frightened me! I was watching some little mice.' Then she showed me what she was looking at. It was a nest of baby mice with their mother.

Exercise 3
1. b   2. a   3. a   4. c   5. c   6. a

Exercise 4
2 3 1 4, 7 5 8 6, 10 12 11 9

Exercise 5
ANSWER: One
(All the others are walking away from St Ives.)

Exercise 6
Open exercise

Exercise 7
1. vase   2. alarm clock   3. mirror   4. purse
5. rose   6. finger

15

📼 Speechwork

Pronunciation
Listen and repeat.
/s/ /s/ /s/ ice nice house

Listen and repeat.
/z/ /z/ /z/ eyes size hose

Listen and repeat.
Hasn't he got nice eyes?
Nice eyes? Those eyes are as cold as ice!

Stress
Listen and repeat.
dadi dadi, dadi dadi, dadi dadi
I was WORKing,
THEY were LEAVing,
SHE was GOing

Intonation
Listen and repeat.
'What were you doing/when the alarm rang?
'What were you doing/when the train came?
'What were you doing/when the bus left?

You're from AIP, aren't you?

Language use	Check facts
Grammar	Question tags:
	positive main clause + negative tag:
	You're English, aren't you?
	He lives here, doesn't he?
	You've been here before, haven't you?
	Negative main clause + positive tag:
	You aren't English, are you?
	He doesn't live here, does he?
	You haven't been here before, have you?
Vocabulary	autograph feed
	cafeteria roam
	captivity cruel
	dolphin daily
	killer whale
	licensed bar
	parrot
	reserve
	sea lion

Background notes

Safari Park   A kind of zoo where most of the animals are not kept in small cages but are left free to roam in fenced reserves. Visitors drive through the animal reserves.

'Big Cats'   An informal expression which refers to all the large members of the cat family, e.g. lions, tigers, leopards, cheetahs, jaguars.

George Michael A famous British pop star.

Presentation

Talk to the students for a few minutes and incorporate some realistic question tags, e.g. before you write the date on the board, say: *It's (Tuesday 15th) today, isn't it?* As you check the register: *(Ruth)'s not here today, is she? There aren't any students away from school today, are there? Ah, (John) you weren't here yesterday, were you?* Before you take in the homework: *I asked you to do Exercise 2 for homework, didn't I?*

Refer students back to each example of a question tag and highlight the form, meaning and intonation. Explain, for example, that you are almost sure John was not here yesterday and that you just want to check. It is not the same as a real question. Question tags are used when we are almost sure of the answer. Point out that a positive sentence takes a negative question tag and a negative sentence takes a positive question tag. Get the students to repeat your examples in chorus, paying attention to the

falling intonation, e.g: *isn't it?*

Note: Most question tags have a falling intonation.

When a question tag has a rising intonation, e.g: *isn't it?*, it is more like a real question because it means we are not so sure of the answer.

Write examples of question tags in different tenses and with different pronouns on the board. Take the examples from your presentation if possible. Point out to students that the question tags are formed with the auxiliaries *be, have, do* or with a modal, e.g: *will, must, should, can.* Thus a main clause in the past simple makes its question tag with *did*, a main clause in the present perfect forms its question tag with *has/have*, etc.

Advertisement

Tell the students what a safari park is (see Background notes). Ask them if they have been to a safari park or zoo and what animals they saw. Teach any vocabulary for names of animals that the students want to know. Introduce the names of the animals and other new vocabulary referred to in the advertisement, e.g: *killer whale, dolphin, sea lion, bird of prey*, etc. Write this focus question on the board: *What would you like to see at Windsor Safari Park?* The students then read the advertisement and tell each other their answer to the focus question in pairs. Ask a few students to give their answers to the class. The students read the advertisement again and answer the questions in the Students' Book.

Dialogue and Exercise 1

Write a focus question on the board: *Why is Rick at Windsor Safari Park?* Play the dialogue and check the answer to the focus question. Explain any unknown vocabulary. The students then discuss the answers to the questions in Exercise 1 in pairs. Play the dialogue again if necessary. Check their answers. Students listen again and repeat. Point out the falling intonation pattern of the question tags.

Exercise 2

Ask the students to study the example sentences in the Look! box. Ask them to tell you how question tags are made. Do Number 1 of the exercise with the whole class and then students work on their own.

Exercise 3

Ask the students in the L1 when question tags are used. If necessary, point out again that they are used to check facts that we are nearly sure of.

Tell the students that you want to check some information for the school records to make sure that they are up to date. Have a piece of paper in your hand to make this seem more realistic. Ask a few students questions to confirm facts you are fairly sure of, e.g: *You live in . . ., don't you? You're (fifteen) now, aren't you?* The students then look at Exercise 3 and write down four things they know, or think they know, about their partner. Check that they understand the noun *taste*. Elicit an example dialogue T–S–S, e.g:

T: (David), how old do you think (Bob) is?
S1: Fifteen.
T: Ask him.
S1: You're fifteen, aren't you (Bob)?
S2: Yes, I am./No, I'm not.
The students then work in pairs.

Exercise 4
Elicit the first two lines of the dialogue from the class and then ask the students to work on their own. When they have finished they can practise reading out their dialogues in pairs.

MODEL ANSWER
YOU: You're George Michael, aren't you?
GEORGE: Yes, that's right, I am.
YOU: Great. Could you sign my autograph book, please?
GEORGE: Yes, sure.
YOU: You're doing a concert in . . . next week, aren't you?
GEORGE: Yes, I am.
YOU: Good. I'm going to get a ticket for it. Thanks for the autograph. Goodbye.

 Oral exercises 1 and 2

Extra activities

1. Names of animals
Put students into teams of three or four. Give them a few minutes to write in English the names of all the animals they can think of. The team with the longest list wins.

2. Find the right tag
Write ten examples of question tags on a sheet of paper. Include a number of different tenses and pronouns. Make one copy for approximately every four students. Cut them up so that each main clause and each tag is on a separate piece of paper. Divide the students into teams of about four. Give each team a set of clauses and tags in mixed order. The first team to match them all together correctly is the winner.

Activity Book Key

Exercise 1
1. shop assistant   2. ticket inspector
3. policewoman   4. hotel clerk
5. doctor   6. pop star

Exercise 2
1. aren't they?   2. haven't they?   3. does he?
4. isn't he?   5. hasn't he?   6. is he?

Exercise 3
1. Yes, he has.   2. Yes, I do.   3. No, she isn't.
4. No, I haven't.   5. Yes, I did.   6. Yes, I am.

Exercise 4
Open exercise

Language use	Ask and talk about frequency of present routines
Grammar	Adverbial phrases of time, *one/two/three hour(s) a day once/twice/three times a week every day/week*: How often do you play basketball? I play *once/twice/three times a week*.
Vocabulary	church blink dentist approximately gym class on average health human hygiene

Materials
A picture of a sportsperson.

Presentation
Introduce the topic by asking students what they did at the weekend, what they usually do in their spare time and how often they do it. Provide any vocabulary that the students want to know to describe their spare-time activities. Show the students the picture of a sportsperson. Write up a two-week diary for this person on the board, e.g:

Monday Training 10–1	Swimming 3.00	
Tuesday Training 10–1		
Wednesday Training 10–1		
Thursday Training 10–1	Swimming 3.00	
Friday Training 10–1		
Saturday Training 10–1	Match 2.30	Restaurant 8.00
Sunday		

(Continue down the board and write up the same programme for the second week.) Explain *to spend time on something* and *to go training*.

Ask the students about the sportsperson's diary, e.g: *How often does he/she go training?* (Six days a week.) *How much time does he/she spend on it?* (Three hours a day.) The students may use short answers when they reply, e.g: *Six days a week* but give them a full sentence to repeat when they repeat in chorus.

Then ask the students to study the Look! box and to use it to help them write sentences about the sportsperson.

Exercise 1
Ask a few example questions from the questionnaire T–S. Point out that students can use a short answer in their reply, e.g:
T: How often do you go swimming?
s: I go once a week./Once a week.
Students read the questionnaire. Explain any unknown vocabulary. Put the students into pairs to do the exercise.

Exercise 2
Ask a student to tell you about her/his partner's activities. Choose one section from the questionnaire for the student to tell you about. Ask the class to help the student and to correct mistakes if necessary. Write the sentences on the board to provide a model for the students. Also direct the students' attention to the model in the book. The students then write about their own partner in the same way.

Did you know?
Explain *blink* and *approximately*. Ask the students how many times a minute they think humans blink. Students then look at their books to find out. Students in pairs can then count the number of times their partner blinks in one minute. The class can compare their findings.

 Oral exercise 3

Extra activities

1. Letter to a fan club/supporters' club
Ask the students to write to the fan club of a sports personality or the supporters' club of a team and find out their training schedule and diet. They can do this in their own language. If they have an interest in an English-speaking team and know the address of the fan club, they can write in English. The students put any information they receive, translated into English, in their project books.

2. Keep a diary

Ask the students to keep a detailed diary in English
for a week and to record how long they spend on
activities. The students can then compare their
diaries in groups in class, e.g:

s1: How often did you watch television last week?
s2: I watched it every day.

Activity Book Key

Exercise 1
1. She's fourteen.
2. the British 100 Metres Freestyle Championship.
3. Yes.
4. swim – every day
   run – three times a week
   train in the gym – twice a week
   have toast and eggs for breakfast – every day
   visit the doctor – once a month
   go out in the evenings – twice a week

Exercise 2
Open exercise

Language use	Talk about degrees of liking and preference
Grammar	*would rather* + infinitive without *to*: *I would/I'd rather watch 'Miami Vice'.* *I would/I'd rather watch comedies than documentaries.* Verbs *like, enjoy, prefer* + noun: *I quite like 'Taxi'.* + gerund (*-ing* form): *I prefer watching sports programmes.*
Vocabulary	channel broadcast comedy popular crime series recent documentary nature programme quiz programme soap opera survey total variety show

Background notes

soap opera A continuing television or radio story about the lives and problems of imaginary characters. 'Dallas' and 'Dynasty' are American soap operas about the lives of very rich families. 'EastEnders' (in Exercise 6) is a British soap opera about a community of ordinary working-class people living in the east end of London.

Presentation

Introduce the topic and revise *like/enjoy* + noun/ gerund by asking the students if they watched television last night, what programmes they watched and what programmes they like. Teach vocabulary for types of TV programmes, as listed in Exercise 4.

Choose a type of programme which you know is popular with your students and a type of programme which is unpopular. Ask the students which one they like better and then introduce the model sentences: *I prefer watching films to the news. I would rather watch films than the news.* Students repeat the sentences in chorus. Point out that:

- *prefer* is followed by a gerund or a noun
- we say we prefer one thing *to* another
- *I would rather* is often shortened to *I'd rather*
- *rather* is followed by the infinitive without *to*

- we say we would rather do one thing *than* another
- the weak form pronunciation of *than* is /ðən/.

Check the students' understanding of the model sentences again by asking: *Which one do you like better?* Elicit other example sentences from the students by writing a list on the board of types of television programmes and asking students to make sentences, e.g: *I'd rather watch comedy programmes than variety shows.* Students repeat each example sentence.

Text and Exercise 1

With books closed, write the questions from Exercise 1 on the board. Explain *channel* and *broadcast*. Ask students what they think the answers are. The students then open their books and read to find out if they were correct. Check the answers to the questions.

Ask the students to explain *Approximately 95 per cent of homes . . .* and *According to a recent survey . . .* Clarify the meanings for them if necessary.

Exercise 3

Ask the students to look at the paragraph about television again and to give you the same sort of information about television in their country. If they do not know the figures, ask them to guess. Then ask students to write this in a paragraph.

Exercise 4

Give the students a little time to write down the names of their favourite programmes and to study the Look! box. Ask them questions about what they like and encourage them to use the language in the Look! box. Refer them to the model exchange. Students then discuss TV programmes in pairs.

Exercise 5

After the group activity, the whole class can compare each group's list of three and work out which are the three most popular programmes in the class.

Exercise 6

Before students listen to the tape, write a focus question on the board: *What types of television programmes do Chloe and Nicky talk about?* Elicit from the students a list of the different types of television programmes and write this list on the board. The students can then note down from the list the programmes that Chloe and Nicky talk about. Play the tape once for students to answer the focus question. Students then copy the chart and fill in what they can. Before the second listening, explain what 'EastEnders' is (see Background notes) and elicit the names of any current popular soap operas.

Play the tape again for students to complete the chart. Students then compare their notes in pairs. Play the tape for a third time if necessary. Ask the students to tell you about Chloe and Nicky, putting their information into sentences.

TAPESCRIPT
Listen to Chloe and Nicky talking about watching television. Look at your book and complete the information in the chart.

INTERVIEWER: Chloe, can you tell me, how much television do you watch a week?
CHLOE: Um . . . 'bout an hour every night, which is about seven hours a week.
INTERVIEWER: What sort of programmes do you like watching?
CHLOE: I like films . . . um . . . mainly, but I like soap operas as well like 'EastEnders' and things, and 'Dallas' and 'Dynasty'.
INTERVIEWER: Do you ever watch quiz programmes or variety shows? What do you think of them?
CHLOE: I think they're very boring – most of the quiz programmes.
INTERVIEWER: And what do you say is your favourite programme, um, of all at the moment? What's the favourite one that you watch at the moment?
CHLOE: 'EastEnders'

INTERVIEWER: Nicky, can you tell me, how much television do you watch a week?
NICKY: More than I should – a lot more than I should – I'd say I watch about two hours a day, mainly when I come home from school because that's when all the programmes I like are on.
INTERVIEWER: How long are you allowed to watch, I mean what time do you have to go to bed?
NICKY: I have to go to bed about . . . um . . . not later than half past ten, but if, say, if there's a very good film on, then I could watch later than that if I wanted to.
INTERVIEWER: Are films your . . . your favourite type of TV programme, or what do you like best?
NICKY: Well, mainly films are my favourite type – that's the ones I watch the most.
INTERVIEWER: And what about sport?
NICKY: Um, yes I . . . I do like sport. I watch sport a lot at the weekends because . . . um . . . rather strange, I like, um, motor racing.

Oral exercises 4 and 5

Extra activities

1. Planning a TV schedule
Tell the students that they are the directors of a TV company. They broadcast from 6.30 am to 9.00 am and from 4.00 pm to midnight Mondays to Fridays. At the weekends they broadcast non-stop all day. They must decide what types of programmes to

broadcast at what time. They must plan a schedule for one or two days, stating what types of programmes will be shown at what hours. Refer the students back to the list in Exercise 4 and ask them if they can think of any other programmes to add to the list, e.g. chat shows, children's programmes, music, game shows, current affairs programmes. Put the students into groups to plan and write their schedules. The discussion should incorporate practice of the language of frequency introduced in Lesson 17 as well as the vocabulary learnt in this lesson, e.g: *I think we should have the news three times a day.*

2. Planning a holiday
Tell the students that they are going on holiday with their parents and grandparents. They must choose a holiday which they would all quite like. First divide the class into three groups: teenage children, parents and grandparents, and ask them to discuss what type of holiday they would like. Then put the students into groups of three to six with one or two teenagers, parents and grandparents in each group and ask them to discuss the holiday and try and reach an agreement. The discussion should include examples of the structures in this lesson, e.g: *I'd rather go to a small village than a big town, I prefer the mountains to the sea.*

Activity Book Key

Exercise 1
TAPESCRIPT
Look at your book. Listen to the advertisements for future TV programmes. Write the name of the programme, the time you can see it, and what kind of programme it is.

1.
On Thursday, 'Hometown' is back! The most popular series since 'Dallas' is returning to your screens! Find out what is happening in Oregon Oil. Check out the ups and downs of the Barker family – their loves, their argument, their fights!
'This time, BJ, you've gone too far!'
Join BJ and the Barkers in 'Hometown', Thursdays at 7.30!

2.
This nuclear explosion was at a test site in Australia. In London, it might have killed four million people. Twenty per cent of Britain's electricity comes from nuclear power stations. Are they completely safe? Or could they explode like a nuclear bomb? We have some facts that will make you think again about nuclear power. That's on 'The Future is Now', tonight at ten o'clock.

3.

VOICE 1:	We've got to move tonight, sir! If we don't take them tonight, they'll be out of the country by tomorrow!
VOICE 2:	For the last time, James, if we arrest Robinson, then we miss the chance of getting the big operators. And I am not going to let you ruin the biggest police operation this year because of your personal problems!
ANNOUNCER:	'The Gang'. 9.45. Tonight.

4.

CHORUS::	'Happy Families!' 'Happy Families!'
ANNOUNCER:	Melanie and James don't have the best luck in the world, and they're not very good at sports. When they try their hand at windsurfing, the results can be hilarious!
MELANIE:	Whooooaaaa!
ANNOUNCER:	Don't miss it, 7.45 tonight, 'Happy Families!' on Channel 6. It's the funniest show on TV!

KEY
1. Hometown – 7.30 – soap opera
2. The Future is Now – 10.00 – documentary
3. The Gang – 9.45 – crime series
4. Happy Families – 7.45 – comedy

Exercise 2
1. She'd rather go on holiday with her parents than with her school.
2. She'd rather go on a cycling holiday than a coach touring holiday.
3. She'd rather have holidays in different places than in the same place every year.

Exercise 3
Open exercise

Exercise 4
ADJECTIVES: interesting, good, frightening, intelligent
NOUNS: programme, documentary, channel, series

LESSON 19 Dolphins in captivity

Language use	Contrast facts
Grammar	Clauses of concession with *although*: *Although dolphins in the wild usually live for more than thirty years, in captivity most die young.* Adverb of contrast *however*: *Dolphins in the wild usually live for more than thirty years. However, in captivity, most die before their twelfth birthday.*
Vocabulary	entertainer blow habitat perform human being shorten lifespan survive mammal commercial myth healthy pool intelligent space although species basically sunglasses however trick rarely trumpet sense of fun

Background notes

limerick (AB) A humorous verse of five lines. The first, second and fifth lines rhyme and the third and fourth lines rhyme.

Read and answer

Ask the students what they know about dolphins and killer whales. After eliciting a few suggestions put the students into groups of three or four and ask them to write a list of things they know about dolphins and killer whales and a list of things they are not sure about and would like to know. A member of each group then reads its list to the rest of the class. Students discuss their queries.

Explain any vocabulary which they may need and introduce some of the new vocabulary which appears in the text. The students then read the text to check their facts and to see if they can find the answers to their own questions and those in the Students' Book. Any information which students cannot find in the text they should try to find for homework.

Ask students to read the text again and to try to deduce the meaning of unknown vocabulary from the context. Check through the new vocabulary with the whole class and explain the meaning where necessary.

Presentation

Ask the students how long dolphins live in the wild and how long they live in captivity. Write the sentences on the board: *Dolphins in the wild usually live for more than thirty years. In captivity, most dolphins die before their twelfth birthday.* Point out to students that the information in the second sentence is surprising after the information given in the first sentence. Say that we need another word to contrast these two facts. The students may suggest *but*. Accept this as correct and then elicit or provide *however* and *although*. Ask the students to study the examples in the Look! boxes. Point out, in the L1 if necessary, that:

- *however* is used to introduce the second contrasting fact. It is used in a separate sentence
- it usually comes at the beginning of a sentence
- it is followed by a comma
- *although* can introduce the first or second piece of information. In the Look! example it introduces the first piece of information
- when we use *although* the two pieces of information are written in one sentence and they are divided by a comma.

Exercise 1

Tell the students that they must decide which two sentences go together. Ask them to put *however* at the beginning of the second sentence, e.g: *1. Killer whales can live for many years in the wild. However, in captivity, most die young.*

Exercise 2

Example: *1. Although killer whales can live for many years in the wild, in captivity, most die young.*

Exercise 3

Ask the students to refer back to the reading passage to make their notes. Point out that they do not need to use full sentences in the notes. Explain any unknown vocabulary in the outline given. Check the finished notes with the whole class. Students then write the article, following the order of the notes. They should try to use only their notes and not refer back to the reading passage again.

Extra activities

1. Find out about another animal

Ask the students to find out about another animal (mammal, bird, fish or reptile) which they are interested in and to write an article about it. The students can also give talks to the class about the animal. The students can do their research from books or go to a local zoo and talk to someone there.

2. Animal quiz

Put the students into teams and ask them to prepare ten questions about animals, e.g: *Where do crocodiles come from? How long do tortoises live?* The teams then play against each other. If possible, the class should have access to an encyclopedia to check any disputed facts.

Activity Book Key

Exercise 1
1. dolphin   2. sunglasses   3. trumpet   4. pool
5. seal   6. scientist

Exercise 2
1. Although the animals sometimes look miserable, they're quite happy.
2. Although Andy doesn't get much money, he likes working with animals.
3. Although he likes working here, he isn't going to stay very long.
4. Although I like animals, I'm not going to work here.
5. Although the animals are happy here, I don't really like zoos.
6. Although it's a long way from here, it's a good job and I like it.

Exercise 3
Blue – zoo – six – tricks – you

Exercise 4
Open exercise

Vocabulary	stage	fluently
	relax	
Speechwork	Pronunciation: /θ/ thin, /t/ tin	
	Stress: da da dida, THREE TIMES a WEEK	
	Intonation:	
	'You're from Dover,/aren't you?	
	You 'aren't from Dover,/are you?	

Background notes

All Fools' Day or April Fools' Day (AB) This is 1st April. People play tricks on each other and try to make one another believe things that are not true. If a trick is played on you, you are an April Fool. It finishes at twelve o'clock midday.

Guy Fawkes' Night (AB) This takes place on the night of 5th November. People have fireworks and they make fires ('bonfires') in their gardens. They often cook potatoes and chestnuts in the fire.

Hallowe'en (AB) See Background notes Lesson 12.

Roleplay

Ask the students to read the information about Sabina and answer any questions they may have. Explain *fluently*. Do the first four lines of the roleplay T–S then put the students into pairs. Ask them to change roles when they have completed the roleplay. At the end, the class can listen to one or two pairs doing the roleplay and correct any mistakes.

 Listen

Explain the context of the interview with books closed. Ask the students to listen particularly for the questions which the interviewer asks. Play the tape once and ask the class what the interviewer wanted to know. Check the answers orally. The students then open their books and read the listening task. Check that they understand all the vocabulary. Play the tape a second time and ask the students to make notes. Pause the tape briefly before *And right now you're doing comedy, aren't you?* to give students the chance to note down the parts which the actor has played. At the end, ask students to compare their answers in pairs and then check through them with the whole class.

Play the tape once again and stop after each of the three question tags. Point out that the first two have a rising intonation pattern. Explain that this is because the interviewer is unsure about the answer. There is something about the appearance of the TV

actor which suggests to the interviewer that she was not expected. The rising question tags show her uncertainty and concern. The third question tag has a slightly falling intonation pattern. Ask the students to repeat the question tags from the tape.

TAPESCRIPT

Listen to this interview with a TV actor. Look at your book and make notes.

INTERVIEWER:	Hello, I'm the reporter from 'Discoveries'. You are expecting me, aren't you?
FRANK:	Yes, do come in. Sit down.
INTERVIEWER:	Thanks. This isn't a bad time to come, is it?
FRANK:	Oh, no, no. Well, I'm always busy but I have a few moments to spare right now.
INTERVIEWER:	Great. Now Frank Wilde, you're what I would call a professional TV actor. You've been in TV series for years now. How long is it exactly?
FRANK:	Er, ten years to be precise.
INTERVIEWER:	That's some time. Do you still enjoy your work or are you getting a bit tired of it?
FRANK:	Oh, no, no, I still enjoy it thoroughly. Every part I do is different. It's always challenging. I've been a policeman in a crime series, a doctor in a hospital drama . . . um . . .
INTERVIEWER:	And right now you're doing comedy, aren't you?
FRANK:	Yes, er, yes, it's a comedy series about a man who marries again and it's called 'Second Time Round'. I've just found out I'm quite good at making people laugh. I never thought I would be, but now people stop me in the street and say: 'Aren't you that funny man from "Second Time Round"?'
INTERVIEWER:	And how do you like to relax?
FRANK:	Well when I get the time, which isn't often, I like packing a rucksack and going walking in the hills. Sometimes I take my eldest son, Jack, with me. He likes getting out of town too. But believe it or not, I also like watching television!

Write

Elicit the first sentence from the class and write it on the board. Ask the students to copy it down and complete the paragraph. Ask a few students to read out their paragraphs and correct any mistakes.

MODEL ANSWER

I have worked in TV for ten years and I enjoy it very much. I've been a policeman in a crime series, a doctor in a hospital drama, and now I'm in a comedy series. When I want to relax I like going walking in the hills.

Game

Explain the 'hot seat' (when one person has the responsibility for making difficult decisions or answering difficult questions). Demonstrate the game by putting yourself in the 'hot seat' first. Encourage students to use question tags with a falling intonation pattern when they are checking information they are reasonably sure of. You could divide the class into groups to play the game to give more of them the opportunity to be in the 'hot seat'.

Dictionary skills
Explain *adverb*, *pronoun*, *preposition* and *conjunction* by giving examples or translating into the L1. The students then do the exercise on their own.

Grammar summary
Remind students that:
- the auxiliary verb in the question tag must agree with the tense of the verb in the main sentence
- *I'd rather* is an abbreviation of *I would rather*
- *would rather* is followed by the infinitive without *to*
- when we use *however*, the two facts to be contrasted are usually written in two sentences and when we use *although*, they are written in one sentence.

Extra activities

1. Guess the actor
Tell the students they are all famous actors and actresses. They must each decide who they want to be and keep it a secret. The students then move around the class talking to each other and asking each other questions to find out who they are. The students answer the questions as if they were the actor, but they must not give their names, e.g:
S1: Where do you come from?
S2: The United States.
S1: And what sort of parts do you play?
S2: For many years I was a cowboy in westerns but now I act in all kinds of films.
The student who discovers the most identities is the winner.

2. Dictionary game
To play this game, each student must have a dictionary. The teacher calls out a word and the students must find the word in the dictionary as quickly as possible. The first student to find the word calls out the page number and then reads the definition.

Activity Book Key

Exercise 1
1. T 2. F 3. T 4. T 5. F 6. T 7. T 8. F

Exercise 2
1. aren't you? 2. isn't it? 3. haven't you?
4. hasn't she? 5. don't they? 6. don't you?
7. wasn't she? 8. isn't he?

Exercise 3
1. Although she likes studying languages, she thinks English is rather difficult.
   She likes studying languages. However, she thinks English is rather difficult.
2. Although I enjoy watching TV, I don't like horror films.
   I like watching TV. However, I don't like horror films.
3. Although he's very shy, he has a lot of friends.
   He's very shy. However, he has a lot of friends.
4. Although I'm sometimes rather moody, I'm normally quite good-tempered.
   I'm sometimes rather moody. However, I'm normally quite good-tempered.

Exercise 4
1. All Fools' Day/April Fools' Day
2. autumn
3. Guy Fawkes' Night
   Hallowe'en
   All Fools' Day/April Fools' Day
4. a) Hallowe'en
   b) All Fools' Day/April Fools' Day
   c) Guy Fawkes' Night

Exercise 5
Open exercise

Exercise 6
ADVERBS: 1. fast 4. clearly 6. well
ADJECTIVES: 2. good 3. brave 5. hot

Speechwork

Pronunciation
Listen and repeat.
/θ/ /θ/ /θ/ thin three thick

Listen and repeat.
/t/ /t/ /t/ tin tree tick

Listen and repeat.
Put a thick tick next to number three.
That's a very thick tree.

Stress
Listen and repeat.
da da dida, da da dida, da da dida
THREE TIMES a WEEK,
TWELVE TIMES a YEAR,
FOUR TIMES a MONTH

Intonation
Listen and repeat.
'You're from Dover,/aren't you?
'She's from London,/isn't she?
'He's a student,/isn't he?

Listen and repeat.
You 'aren't from Dover,/are you?
She 'isn't from London,/is she?
He 'isn't a student,/is he?

It may hurt a little.

Language use	Ask and talk about degrees of possibility
Grammar	Modal verbs *may* (possibility), *will/won't* (definite future): *It may/will/won't hurt.* Reflexive pronouns: *He/She'll hurt himself/herself.*
Vocabulary	athlete · break · bread knife · burn · bronze · fall over · character · hurt · dentist · knock over · drill · afterwards · filling · definitely · injection · possibly · lead (electric) · wide · medal · I'm afraid · saucepan · Be careful! · vacuum cleaner

Presentation

Think of a future event that is of interest to the students. (See Exercise 3 for some ideas.) Talk briefly to the students about it and incorporate an example of *will, won't* and *may* in what you say, e.g. talking about a forthcoming football match: *It will be an exciting match on Saturday. Who do you think will win? I think (Manchester United) may win this time. I think all the tickets have been sold so it won't be possible to buy a ticket on Saturday.*

Alternatively, write a paragraph incorporating the structures and read it out to the students. Whichever approach you choose, extract the examples of the structure from what you said. Explain that *will* and *won't* are more definite than *may*. Write the examples on the board. Point out that:

- *will* is often contracted to *'ll*
- *will not* is often contracted to *won't*
- *will, won't* and *may* refer to the future
- they are all followed by the infinitive without *to*
- *will* and *may* are often used after *I think . . .*, e.g. *I think they'll win*
- the negative *I don't think they will . . .* is much more common than *I think they won't . . .*

Ask students to study the Look! box. Explain that the sentences in the right-hand column have the same meaning as the sentences in the left-hand column. Elicit from the students more sentences about the event you have discussed, using *may, will* or *won't*. Or give the students another forthcoming event to talk about.

Dialogue and Exercise 1

Ask students to look at the picture and tell you what is happening. Ask them if they have been to the dentist recently, how often they go and if they like going. Teach a set of vocabulary on the theme, including the vocabulary from the dialogue.

Write a focus question on the board: *What treatment did Kate have at the dentist?*

With books closed, play the tape and check the answer to the question. Ask the students to look at the true or false questions in Exercise 1 and to discuss them in pairs. Ask them not to read the dialogue yet. Play the tape a second time so that the students can check their answers. Students then listen to the paused version of the dialogue and repeat.

Exercise 2

Introduce/revise vocabulary for the names of the items in the picture, e.g: *saucepan, vacuum cleaner, bread knife, electric lead, glass, stool.* The students look at the picture. Ask them why it has the title: *Your kitchen may not be as safe as you think!* The students then tell you what is dangerous in the kitchen and why, e.g: *The glasses are dangerous because the little boy may break them and cut himself.*

As you elicit from the students what is dangerous and why, introduce the verbs in the box. Then put the students into pairs to list what may happen to the little boy, e.g: *He may knock over the saucepan and burn himself.*

Exercise 3

Ask the students to read the list of topics and the example exchange. Explain any unknown vocabulary. *Athletes* in Number 1 refers to all sportspeople taking part in the Olympics, not just those taking part in the athletics. *The athletics* in the example exchange refers to walking, running, throwing and jumping competitions.

Choose one of the topics as an example and ask a question to elicit some comments from the students, e.g: *'Dallas' is on TV tonight. Do you think JR will leave his wife?* etc. Prompt students into using *may, will* and *won't* in their replies. Put them into pairs or groups to talk about two of the topics. Add to the list any other topics which you think your students would be interested in.

Exercise 4

The students write the dialogue on their own and then practise reading it aloud in pairs. Suggest that they may want to extend the dialogue and provide a beginning and an end.

MODEL ANSWER

DENTIST: I need to take out a tooth.
YOU: Will it hurt?
DENTIST: No, it won't hurt with an injection but it may hurt a little afterwards.
YOU: Will the injection hurt?
DENTIST: No, it won't. You'll just feel a little pain at first but then you won't feel anything.
YOU: OK.

Oral exercise 1

Extra activities

1. Tell your fortune

Tell the students they are fortune tellers. Someone has come to see them to find out about their future. They must write the fortunes on a sheet of paper in three sentences: one sentence with *will*, one with *may* and one with *won't*, e.g: *You will marry when you are 25. You may be rich. You won't have any children.* Ask all the students to fold up their papers and to drop them into a box. Shake the box up and pass it round. Each student must pick out a piece of paper to find out their fortune. Ask the students to tell the class what their fortune is, e.g: *I may live in England*, etc.

2. Picture from memory

Show the students a picture of a kitchen from a magazine. Hold up the picture for about five seconds. The students then make notes of what they can remember about the kitchen. They should list what was in it and, if possible, where it was, e.g: *There was a knife on the table*. The students then compare their notes in groups and draw up a new list of all the information from the group. One member of each group reads it out to the class. Show the picture again and then the class can check the differences between their notes and the picture.

Activity Book Key

Exercise 1

A: Are you going to the disco tonight?
B: I don't know. I'm a bit tired. I may go.
A: Robbo's going to be there.
B: Really? Will he definitely be there?
A: Oh, yes, he'll definitely be there. He told me today.
B: How about Karen? Will she be there?
A: No, she won't. Robbo told me that, too.
B: That means we won't see her tonight?
A: No, but we may/will/'ll see her before we go.

Exercise 2

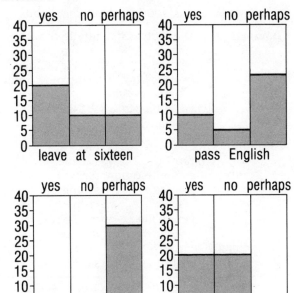

Exercise 3

1. I think twenty students/people in my class will leave when they are sixteen and ten will stay. The rest may leave.
2. I think ten of us will pass the English exam and five will fail. The rest may pass.
3. I think five people/students will pass Geography/the Geography exam and five people/students will fail. The rest may pass.
4. Half of us will pass Maths/the Maths exam and the rest will fail.

Boys used to wear caps.

Language use	Ask and talk about past habits
Grammar	The verb *used* + infinitive with *to*: *Did you use to watch 'Playschool'?* *I used to like swimming but I don't now.* *I didn't use to watch 'Ready! Steady! Go!'*
Vocabulary	brickyard pie cap seaside communication servant disease swimmer eel taste family life transport horse-drawn twopence coach poor leisure slum

Background notes

eel-and-meat pie   A traditionally cheap food, which used to be particularly popular in working-class areas of London.

twopence   This is twopence in pre-decimal currency and is equivalent to less than one penny.

slum children   A slum is a house or an area of houses in very bad condition and 'slum children' are the children who live in them.

Materials

A picture of a young man or woman, obviously rich.

Presentation

Show the class the picture of a rich young man or woman. Give the person a name, e.g: *Nigel*. Build up a picture of a rich lifestyle, eliciting ideas from the students where possible, e.g: *He's a rich businessman. He lives in a luxury flat in the centre of town and he has a big house in the country. In the evenings, he goes to expensive restaurants and night clubs. He likes champagne and expensive food. He drives a Mercedes. He goes sailing in the summer and skiing in the winter.*

Then tell the students that his picture was in fact taken a few years ago. Draw or stick prison bars over the picture and tell the students that he is in prison. Ask them about his lifestyle now, what he eats, what he drinks, how he spends his day. Compare his life now with his life in the past, e.g: *He drinks water with his dinner now, but before he went to prison he drank champagne.* Give an example sentence, e.g: *He used to drink champagne.* Check students' understanding. Elicit other example sentences and get students to repeat them in chorus.

Lead into an example of the negative, e.g: *He gets up at half-past five now. Before he went to prison, he usually got up at about ten o'clock. He didn't use to get up at half-past five.* Elicit one or two more examples of the negative and get students to repeat them.

Present the question form by telling students that a reporter from a local newspaper has come to interview the prisoners about their lives before they came into prison. Elicit some example questions from the students, e.g: *Where did you use to live?* Put the students into pairs to act out a conversation between the reporter and Nigel.

Write examples of the positive, negative and question forms on the board for students to copy. Draw a time-line.

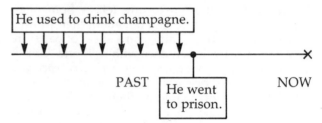

Point out, in the L1 if necessary, that:
- *used* + infinitive with *to* describes a situation or habitual event that continued for a period of time in the past but is now finished
- the negative and question forms are made with the auxiliary *did* + *use to*
- the short answer to a *Did you use to . . . ?* question is: *Yes, I did./No, I didn't.*

Pictures and Exercise 1

With books closed, the students tell you what they think life was like at the beginning of this century. Prompt them into using *used to* in their replies. Then with books open, students look at the pictures and describe them. Teach any unknown vocabulary in the exercise, and any other vocabulary which they may want to use. Students read Exercise 1. Point out that they may use negative sentences. Elicit the sentences, e.g: *Poor children didn't use to wear shoes.* Give them more vocabulary if they need it.

Exercise 2

Teach any unknown vocabulary in the exercise. Choose one of the topics to discuss with the whole class and then put the students into small groups of three or four to discuss the rest of the topics. Give each group the opportunity to report back briefly to the class. The structure *used to* should be incorporated into the discussion, e.g: *Poor children used to go to.work when they were very young.* There is no need for the students to use the *used to* structure all the time, however, if they are communicating naturally.

Exercise 3

Ask the students to think of their life a few years ago, at the age of eight for example. Ask how it was different from their life now. Students then read the example exchange and do the exercise in pairs.

Exercise 5

Explain the context of the tape. Elicit from the students a list of spare-time activities and write it on the board. Add to the list any activities on the tape not suggested by the students and explain *interior decorating* and *to paint*. Write the names *Brian* and *Iris* on the board. Ask the students to listen and note down who talks about which activities on the list. Play the tape. Check the students' answers. Before the second playing, ask the students to note down which activities Brian and Iris *used to do* and which activities they do *now*. Check their answers. Students read the task in their books, listen to the tape for a third time and make notes. They can then compare their notes in pairs. When you check the task with the students, encourage them to make *used to* sentences where appropriate.

TAPESCRIPT

Listen to two people talking about their changes in taste. Look at your book and take notes.

INTERVIEWER: Iris, I want to talk about the way that your tastes have changed since you were young. Let's start by talking about what you used to do in your spare time. What did you use to do in your spare time when you were young?

IRIS: Um . . . when I was younger, I used to go dancing quite a lot and to the cinema. Um . . . swimming was another favourite pastime of mine. The cinema, I'd go two or three times a week and dancing once or twice, depending on if I had the money to go. Swimming, I used to have a season ticket regularly and I was quite a good swimmer and . . . er . . . I used to enjoy it.

INTERVIEWER: Do you still like to do dancing, swimming and going to the cinema or do you do different kinds of things now in your spare time?

IRIS: Well now I very rarely go to the cinema. I just don't seem to have the time to go now. Swimming, I only go swimming on holiday, which I think is a pity. Dancing, we still go dancing occasionally so, yes.

INTERVIEWER: What else do you like doing now?

IRIS: I love my home and garden. I love to do my garden if I've got the time and I do find time for that. Other things do get neglected. Um . . . again I like to do interior decorating.

INTERVIEWER: What do you mean by interior decorating?

IRIS: Er, painting and papering. Um . . . in fact I'm a great painter, even though I say it myself.

INTERVIEWER: Brian, when you were young, say, in your teens, what did you use to do in your spare time?

BRIAN: Well, a lot of time was spent . . . er . . . with friends really in the parks, playing football, playing cricket. A lot of my time was taken up with homework, which I'm glad I don't have to do now. I used to play basketball at school but I'm not fit enough to play that any longer. I used to spend some time stamp collecting, although I probably stopped stamp collecting at about age fourteen and then actually picked it up again just about er four or five years ago. And then I suppose when I was about . . . er . . . eighteen I started playing the guitar, and . . . er . . . that developed. I started playing with bands at university and . . . er . . . that interest has grown considerably, and I spend quite a lot of time now listening to music . . . er . . . playing in bands and even writing music. Cooking is something that I've really only become interested in in more recent years. Um . . . that's not something that it's easy to do when you're perhaps seventeen or eighteen – not if you're a boy anyway – it's not traditional.

Oral exercises 2 and 3

Extra activities

1. Our town in the past

Ask the students to talk to an elderly relative, friend or neighbour who has always lived in their home town. Ask them to find out what has changed in the town and to write about the changes in their project books. They can do this individually or the class can do it as a project. Ask them to find some old photographs or to copy or draw some.

2. The time machine

Tell the students that they are going in a time-machine into the future and they will not be coming back. Ask them what they will take with them into the future. This may include things which are of personal value to the students and things which would be of interest and benefit to a future society. Elicit ideas from the class and write them on the board. Then tell the students that they can only take a fixed number of these items – four, for example. Put them into pairs to agree on a list of four. When the pairs have agreed, put two pairs together into a group of four and ask them to agree on a list of four, then the groups of four go into eight and then the whole class can try to come to an agreement. This should be a fairly free communicative activity without much correction.

Activity Book Key

Exercise 1
1. There used to be a library in Peter Street but there's a bank there now.
2. There used to be a book shop in Peter Street but there's a TV and radio shop there now.
3. There used to be a toy shop in Hill Street but there's a video shop there now.
4. There used to be a coffee shop in Hill Street but there's a hairdresser's there now.
5. There used to be a butcher's in Richmond Lane but there's a supermarket there now.
6. There used to be a sweet shop in Richmond Lane but there's a hamburger bar there now.

Exercise 2
1. She used to live with her parents but now she lives in the university.
2. She used to play a lot of sport but now she doesn't like sport.
3. She used to have a lot of money but now she doesn't have much money.
4. She didn't use to read many books but now she reads all the time.
5. She didn't use to have many friends/She used to have no friends but now she has a lot of good friends.

Skills	Comprehension, summary and vocabulary skills	
Vocabulary	button	explain
	doorbell	hesitate
	message	point
	parcel	press
	push button	square
	thing	valuable
	tool box	politely
	call	puzzled
	check	someone
	connect	somewhere

Background notes

Literary extract The extract is taken from *Button Button*, a story by Richard Matheson, which is contained in a set of science fiction stories: *2001 and Beyond* in the Longman Simplified English Series.

Read and listen

Pre-teach the essential vocabulary that the students may not be able to deduce from context, e.g: *parcel, square box, push button, press.* The students then listen to the first two paragraphs of the text as they read, up to: '*Mr Steward will call on you at eight o'clock this evening.*' Put the students into pairs or groups to discuss it. Write these questions on the board to guide their discussion: *1. What do you think the small box is? 2. Why has it got a push button on it? 3. Why did they receive the box? 4. Who is Mr Steward?*

The students then report back their ideas to the class. Play the rest of the tape and ask the students to listen as they read and to think about the answers to the first four questions again. When the students have heard/read the rest of the text, add three more questions to the list on the board: *5. What will happen if they press the button? 6. What will Mr Steward give them in return for pressing the button? 7. Do you think they will do it?*

Also write on the board any vocabulary which the students may not know and ask them to try to deduce the meaning from context and then to check it in their dictionaries. Ask the students to discuss all seven questions, and the meanings of the vocabulary. Check the answers to the questions and the vocabulary with the class. Encourage them to discuss what they think will happen. Then tell them the outcome of the story. This is that Mr Lewis does not want to press the button but Mrs Lewis is tempted by the money and accepts. Mr Lewis then dies in an accident. The class can go on to discuss what they think the moral of the story is.

Exercise 1

Ask the students to read the sentences. Explain any unknown vocabulary to them. The students can work on the exercise alone or in pairs.

Exercise 2

Check that the students understand the meaning of the verbs in the box and explain any new vocabulary in the passage. Ask them to do the obvious ones first, e.g: *called, asked, answered.* Point out the question mark and that a question is likely to be followed by an answer.

KEY
called asked answered explained said

Extra activities

1. Jumbled story

Divide the students into groups of eight or nine. Give each student a piece of paper with a short extract from a story on it. Ask the students to read their extracts to each other and to arrange themselves into a line so that the student with the first part of the story is at the beginning of the line and the student with the last part is at the end. When the students have arranged themselves correctly, they should be able to tell the story going from the beginning of the line to the end.

2. The perfect parcel

Ask the students to discuss what they would most like to receive in a parcel in the post.

Activity Book Key

 Exercise 1

TAPESCRIPT
Look at your book and listen to the description. Make notes about the four doors, then choose the correct door to get out of the cave.

NARRATOR:
You can see four doors in front of you by the light of your candle. You have two minutes to decide which door is the way out of the cave. You can listen to the tape twice then your candle will go out. Are you ready? Then I will begin.

There are four doors in front of you, numbered from left: 11, 12, 13 and 14. Each door has a button next to it which opens the door electrically.

You walk up to the doors, and you can see that they are all different. The first – Number 11 – is a beautiful silver door, with pictures of swords and soldiers. The second is even more beautiful, gold, with a gold mirror. Number 13 is an ugly wooden door with a plain wooden handle. Number 14 is stone, with a stone seat next to it.

You sit on the seat and think about your next move. You can remember two things from your map. Firstly, the silver door used to be safe, but now it is dangerous. Secondly, the door with the mirror on it will kill you, because there is a lake behind it. So you have two doors to decide between: the stone door and the wooden one.

You walk over to the stone door and listen. You listen for half a minute, then you can hear something. You can hear a large animal breathing on the other side of the door. Suddenly, you make your decision, run to the other door, press the button, and you escape safely out of the cave.

The question is – which door did you go through?

KEY
Door Number 13: the wooden door

Exercise 2
1. "Would you like some more tea?" he asked.
2. "No, thanks," answered Mrs Broughton, "I've had enough, thank you."
3. "I'll have some, please," called Tina from the kitchen.
4. "You've already got some, haven't you?" he replied.
5. "No," Tina explained, "I had some but I'm afraid I knocked it over."
6. "Oh, Tina!" he said, "You're always doing that!"

Exercise 3
If the students follow the instructions correctly, they will write only their name in the box. (See instruction number 8.)

Nice teeth, nice smile!

Language use	Talk about eating habits Express feelings about unpleasant things Agree and disagree
Grammar	Expressions *can't stand, don't mind, be frightened of* + gerund (*-ing* form); Inversion with *so* and *nor*: *I'm frightened of going* to hospital. *Yes, so am I.* *I don't mind wearing* braces. *Nor do I.* Adverbs *hardly ever, never*: *I hardly ever eat* sweets. *I never drink* milk.
Vocabulary	acid boast adult cause boiled sweet rot braces stare chewing-gum ugly decay (tooth) surprisingly false teeth I can't stand fizzy drink ice-lolly metal peanut smile toffee

Read and answer

Ask the students to tell you what they eat and drink. As they do so, teach any vocabulary that they need. Ask the students to look at the picture and name all the items of food and drink. Help them if necessary. Write all the words on the board and add the names of any other food and drink the students have mentioned. Tell the students to put them into two columns: (1) bad/very bad for your teeth, (2) not very bad for your teeth. The students can do this in pairs.

Pre-teach: *smile* (n.), *decay, to rot (tooth-rotters)*. Ask the students to read the focus questions and to answer them from the text. Check the answers to the questions and explain: *to boast, set of teeth, nowadays, on average, surprisingly, acid*. Ask the students if their two lists corresponded to what was written in the text and encourage them to discuss their reactions to the text.

Exercise 1

The students draw a chart like the one in the model and list all the food and drink in the text. Elicit a few example questions and answers from the students, e.g:

T: (John), ask (Sue) how often she eats cheese.
S1: How often do you eat cheese (Sue)?

S2: Every day.
Teach *hardly ever*. Divide the students into groups to ask each other.

Exercise 2

Ask each group to report on the results of the survey done in Exercise 1. Help them with the language as necessary and prompt them into using *most* and *not many*, e.g: *Most people in this group eat bread every day. Not many people in this group drink milk.*

Presentation

Remind the students of the brief discussion they had on going to the dentist in Lesson 21. Ask them again to tell you if they like going to the dentist or not and lead from this into a presentation of *can't stand* and *don't mind*. e.g: *(Anna) can't stand going to the dentist. (Chris) doesn't mind going to the dentist.* Clarify the meaning and check students' understanding. Point out that:

● *can't stand* is followed by a noun or the gerund
● *STAND* has a strong stress. *DENTist* is also stressed
● *don't mind* is generally used with things that are not pleasant. It means it does not worry or frighten the person. She/He does not find it difficult or horrible. It is followed by a noun or gerund.
● *MIND* and *DENTist* are stressed.

Tell the students not to try to use *stand* and *mind* in the positive. They are only occasionally used in the positive and the concept is very difficult. Drill the example sentences chorally and individually.

Exercise 3

Revise the dental vocabulary taught in Lesson 21 and teach *braces*. (Use the picture of Emma in the Students' Book.) Ask the students to look at the pictures and read the statements. See if they can deduce the meaning of *stares* and *metal*. Answer any other questions on vocabulary. Ask the students to do Exercise 3 on their own or in pairs. Point out that *to be frightened of . . .* is followed by a noun or gerund.

Exercise 4

Write four column headings on the board: *(1) like, (2) don't like, (3) don't mind, (4) can't stand*.

Ask the students to look at the list of prompts in Exercise 4 and check that they understand all the vocabulary. Ask students to make a sentence using one of the column headings. e.g: *I can't stand going to the dentist.* Agree with the student: *No, nor can I.* Elicit a few more sentences and agree using *So* or *Nor*. This should be revision for the students as it was introduced in Students' Book 2.

Remind students that:
- *so* and *nor* are used when we want to say the same about ourselves as the first person has said about her/himself
- *so* is used with positive statements and that *nor* is used with negative statements
- *so* and *nor* are followed by an auxiliary or modal auxiliary verb and then the subject
- the auxiliary or modal auxiliary must agree with the first sentence. For example, if the main verb in the first sentence is in the present simple form, the auxiliary *do* or *does* is used in the reply after *so* or *nor*.

Elicit a few example dialogues S-S with the help of the class and then put the students into pairs.

 Oral exercises 4 and 5

Extra activities

1. Team Game
Divide the students into teams. Give the teams a few minutes to write a list of sentences beginning: *I like/don't like/don't mind/can't stand . . . .* A student from one team then reads a sentence and a student from the other team must answer using *so* or *nor*. Each team gets a point for a correct statement and a correct response. The game must be played at a fast pace and the students should not be given more than a couple of seconds to think of the response.

2. Advice from the dentist
Ask the students to write down everything they ate and drank the previous day. Put them into pairs. They swap their information and take it in turns to roleplay a dentist making comments and giving advice. The dentist must say what she/he thinks of the student's diet and if she/he thinks the student eats too much of something or not enough of something, e.g: *You eat a lot of sandwiches. Cheese sandwiches are good but not jam sandwiches. You shouldn't eat jam, it's very bad for your teeth. And I think you drink too much Coke,* etc.

Activity Book Key

Exercise 1
1.a   2.c   3.a   4.a   5.a   6.c

Exercise 2
1. I'm frightened of going to the dentist.
2. I can't stand dancing.
3. I don't like walking to work.
4. I don't mind visiting my grandparents at the weekend.
5. I hate answering the telephone.
6. I love working in a petrol station.

Exercise 3
1. fizzy   2. eyebrows   3. forest   4. pronoun
5. trumpet

Exercise 4
A: Do you like it here?
B: Well, I like being on holiday but I don't really like living in this camp.
A: Oh? That's interesting. Why don't you like being here?
B: Because it's so cold. I don't mind the food or the other people but I can't stand sleeping in a freezing tent.
A: I'm surprised. I didn't mind sleeping in the cold when I was young, but things were different then.

Vocabulary	accident	perfectly
	childhood	Don't be silly.
	midnight	
	pocket money	
Speechwork	Pronunciation: /eɪ/ say, /e/ said	
	Stress: dida da dadi, I CAN'T STAND SMOKing.	
	Intonation: 'Will it hurt? ↘	
	It 'won't 'hurt much. ↘	

Pictures and conversation

The students briefly look at the pictures and tell you what they think is happening. Ask them if they have disagreements with their parents and what kinds of things they disagree about. The students then read the conversation and find out what the family is arguing about. Point out that they must read from left to right. Check their understanding of the conversation and see if they can guess the meaning of any unknown vocabulary from context.

Roleplay

Ask the students to read the instructions for the roleplay and check that they understand the vocabulary. Elicit a model roleplay from the class and then put the students into pairs to do their own roleplays. After doing the roleplay, students write the conversation.

Listen

Briefly explain the context of the tape. Write the names of all the places mentioned on the tape on the board: *Walworth, South London, Kennington Park, Brighton.*

Ask the students to listen to the questions which the interviewer asks. Play the tape once. Ask the students to tell you what the interviewer's questions were. The students then copy down the task in the box. Point out that they do not need to write the information in full sentences. Play the tape for a second time in sections, giving students time to make notes and check through their answers. At the end, ask the students how old they think Bert is and why they think so. (The clues are: his voice, there was no television, and references to *in those days*.)

The students can then use their information to roleplay the conversation between Bert and the interviewer.

TAPESCRIPT
Listen to this person talking about his childhood. Look at your book and complete the information in the box.

INTERVIEWER: Bert, where were you born and where did you grow up?
BERT: Well, I was born in Walworth, in South London. I grew up in . . . in . . . er . . . Walworth and not only grew up I . . . I was there until the age of twenty-four . . . er . . . this is where I spent my youth and also my schooldays.
INTERVIEWER: Was the school close to your home, or did you have to go a long way to school?
BERT: No, the school actually was about, I should think, about a mile away . . . er . . . which in those days a mile seemed a heck of a way for me to go. But we had to walk to school we didn't have . . . a . . . anycase there was no buses or transport that went that way, so whatever the weather it was a case of getting there and walking there.
INTERVIEWER: What did you use to do in the evenings?
BERT: Well, in the evenings, we used to visit one another's . . . I'm talking now about wintertime when the, the nights were long . . . er . . . we used to visit each other's houses; but in the summer we would walk to Kennington Park, which was about a quarter of an hour away, where we would play cricket . . . er . . . we . . . we were never allowed to go there during the winter because of the dark nights and getting back.
INTERVIEWER: Of course there wasn't any television in those days. Did you play any music or anything like that?
BERT: Yes. This is . . . We had no . . . we had to make our own amusements – not only us, but also our parents. We only had one instrument in those days and that was a piano and we all became accomplished in some form or manner of singing or playing.
INTERVIEWER: What did you use to do for your holidays when you were young?
BERT: Aw, this . . . this was the one time of the year that meant so much. First of all, I think this was because all my people, my relatives, on my mother's side and my father's side, all lived in Brighton. So consequently we went to Brighton every year. Now Brighton itself was in those days a wonderful place. Not like it is now. There were amusements of all sorts. During the day: the beach, the water, swimming; yes, we had everything there. My childhood days at Brighton meant so much to me.

Write

When you have checked the students' sentences, ask them to compare what they have found out. Lead from this into a class or group discussion about the differences between their life now and their parents' life at the same age. Ask them what they think is better now and what was better then.

Dictionary skills
KEY

1. separate	4. successful	7. marriage
2. incredible	5. emigrate	8. receive
3. beautiful	6. rhythm	9. knives

Grammar summary
Remind students that:
- *used* has the form of a past simple verb and questions and negatives are formed with *did + use*. The auxiliary *did* is used in the short answer
- *hardly ever* goes before the main verb (but after the verb *to be*)
- *can't stand* and *don't mind* are followed by the gerund
- the auxiliary or modal auxiliary used after *so* and *nor* must agree with the first sentence.

Extra activities

1. Discussion: the past and the future
Ask the students to remember what they found out about their parents' lives when they were children and teenagers. Put them into groups to compare their lives with their parents' lives at the same age. Encourage them to use *used to* when talking about their parents' early lives. Ask them to list what they think is better and what they think is worse for teenagers now compared to teenagers then. Then ask them to imagine what life will be like for their own children when they are teenagers. Encourage them to use *will* and *may*, e.g: *Our children may not/won't go to the cinema because everyone will have a video recorder.* Point out that the negative of *may* is *may not*.

2. Project: Museum visit
With the students' help, devise a questionnaire to be used in a nearby museum, e.g:
Visit the section on the Romans. Find out:
– what the people used to wear.
– what kind of houses they used to live in.
– what they used to eat.
– how they used to prepare their food.
Ask students to visit the museum and answer the questionnaire. The members of the class can then compare their findings.

Activity Book Key

Exercise 1
1. Perhaps 2. No 3. Yes 4. Perhaps 5. Yes
6. Yes 7. Perhaps

Exercise 2
A: There's my old school. I used to be a student there.
B: Really? Did you use to go to a private school?
A: Yes, I did. I used to sit in one of the classrooms on the first floor.

B: Well, you've never told me that before.
A: No, I used to be embarrassed about it. We had to wear a funny uniform.
B: What? Did you use to wear that uniform with the strange hat?
A: Yes. I didn't use to like it but we had no choice.

Exercise 3
1. called 2. asked 3. replied 4. speak 5. —
6. answering 7. explained

Exercise 4
1. A bird in the hand is worth two in the bush.
2. Better late than never.
3. Look before you leap.
4. You always think the grass is greener on the other side of the fence.

Exercise 5
Open exercise

Exercise 6
Open exercise

Exercise 7
Open exercise

Exercise 8
Open exercise

Speechwork Lessons 21–25

Pronunciation
Listen and repeat.
/eɪ/ /eɪ/ /eɪ/ say wait gate

Listen and repeat.
/e/ /e/ /e/ said wet get

Listen and repeat.
'Wait at the gate,' she said, 'or you'll get wet.'
'What did you say?' he said.

Stress
Listen and repeat.
dida da dadi, dida da dadi, dida da dadi
I CAN'T STAND SMOKing,
They DON'T LIKE WAITing,
I DON'T MIND STAYing.

Intonation
Listen and repeat.
'Will it hurt?

It 'won't 'hurt much.

'Will it be expensive?

It 'won't 'cost much.

Activity Book Key Halfway Roundup

Exercise 1
1. Have you been to many countries?
2. I used to go to the youth club when I was younger but I don't go any more.
3. I'll send you a postcard when I get to Canada.
4. Were they sleeping when you called?
5. I shouted at them and they ran away.
6. We've seen a lot of strange things but we've never seen anything like this before.
7. He used to live here but he moved a year ago.
8. Will she explain if you ask her?

Exercise 2
Open exercise

Exercise 3
NOUNS: director, chess, magazine, success
VERBS: inspect, rob, relax, hitch-hike, accept

Exercise 4
ACROSS 1. brought 4. bet 6. read 7. eaten 8. tear
9. tie 11. left 12. put 15. thrown 16. lie

DOWN 1. burnt 2. understood 3. hurt 4. bent
5. take 10. spent 11. let 13. told 14. flew

Exercise 5
human being, TV channel, sense of humour,
capital letter, pair of sunglasses, building site,
old people's home

Exercise 6
1. 15,452,900 2. About 7,700,000
3. About 2,575,500 4. 140 5. smaller
6. 36,735 km 7. People have lived there for 38,000 years but the Europeans arrived 200 years ago.
8. In winter 9. Australia

If I hit the spaceship . . .

Language use	State consequences
	Make threats
Grammar	First conditional: *if* + clause in present simple + clause in simple future:
	If I hit the spaceship, *I'll stop.*
	If you don't give my money back, *I'll call* the manager.

Vocabulary		
diary	be in trouble
game	Hang on.
object	Leave them
score	alone.
spaceship	Let's get out of
change (money)	here.
give back	Shut up!
miss	What's going
man-made	on?
outer	you lot
	You're nothing
	but trouble.

Presentation

Tell the students that Mrs Andrews is a teacher in England. She is asking her English students about their plans for the weekend. Explain that it is summer but that in England people never know what sort of weather they will have the next day and so they often make plans for the sun and plans for the rain. Divide the board into two columns: *SUN* and *RAIN*. Ask the class to imagine what plans the English students may have for the weekend and write their ideas in the appropriate column. Add some ideas of your own to the lists if the students do not produce many, or prompt more ideas from them using pictures or mime. Do not worry about what structure the students use at this stage. Example lists:

SUN	RAIN
go/beach	go/cinema
have/picnic	go/museum
go/swimming	stay/home
sunbathe	watch/television
go/park	listen/music
play/tennis	visit/friends
sit/garden	read/book

Elicit or provide a model dialogue between Mrs Andrews and one of her students, Vicky, e.g:

MRS ANDREWS: What are your plans this weekend?
VICKY: If the sun shines/If it's sunny, I'll go to the beach, but if it rains, I'll go to the cinema.

Check students' understanding of the structure. Drill the dialogue chorally, with two halves of the class taking a part each, and then individually. Elicit other answers by pointing to prompts on the board and drill each example.

Put the students into pairs to practise questions and answers, using the prompts. Students can then give their own answers about their plans for the weekend. Write up examples of the structure on the board.

Point out that:

- the *if* clause can go first or second in the sentence
- when the *if* clause goes first, it is followed by a comma
- when the simple future (*will*) clause goes first, there is no comma
- the simple future cannot be used in the *if* clause.

 Dialogue

Ask the students if they have ever been to an amusement arcade and if they think they are good or bad things. Teach and practise a set of vocabulary on the theme, including the vocabulary which appears in the dialogue. Ask the students questions about the picture: *Who's in the picture? Where are they? What can you say about the other two boys? What do you think the two boys are going to do?*

Write a focus question on the board: *What do the two boys want?* Play the tape and check the students' answers. Play the tape again, stopping at any new vocabulary or expressions which were not pre-taught. Ask the students what they think the words mean and explain them if necessary. The students then listen to the paused version of the tape and repeat.

Note: *'em* is an abbreviation of *them*. It is sometimes written in direct speech in dialogues or plays to indicate the colloquial weak form.

Exercise 1

Ask students to study the examples in the Look! box. Ask questions to check their understanding. The students then write the completed sentences from Exercise 1 in their notebooks.

Exercise 2

Ask the students to write the complete sentences in their notebooks. Point out that there is often more than one suitable ending.

Exercise 3

Point out to students that they need to use a negative verb in the *if* clause in Number 2.

Example: *1. If she runs, she'll catch the bus. (If she doesn't run, she won't catch the bus.)*

Exercise 4

Check that the students understand the instructions. When they have written the dialogue in their notebooks, ask them to practise reading it aloud in pairs.

MODEL ANSWER
YOU: Give me back my diary, please!
BOY: No, I won't!
YOU: If you give it back, I'll give you some sweets.
BOY: No, I won't.
YOU: OK then. If you give it back, I'll give you some sweets and I'll buy you an icecream.
BOY: All right, here you are.

Did you know?

Ask students to try and find out what some of the objects are.

 Oral exercises 1 and 2

Extra activities

1. Chain story

Give the students a first conditional sentence to start off a story, e.g: *If I go to bed late tonight, I'll wake up late tomorrow morning*. Get them to continue and give them the next sentence as an example, e.g: *If I wake up late tomorrow morning, I'll miss the train*. The students continue in the same way round the class or round their groups. Point out that each sentence must make sense and fit in with the rest of the story. When the story comes to an end, ask a student to provide the first sentence for another one and play the game again.

2. Team game: If you go to London . . .

Explain to the students that a travel agent is giving a customer advice and information about where to go for a holiday. The customer asks about a country or city and the travel agent replies using a sentence in the first conditional. The students are the travel agents. Divide them into teams. Give each team the name of a country or city/town in turn and the team must give some information about it using the first conditional, e.g:
Paris – TEAM 1: If you go to Paris, you'll (be able to) see the Eiffel Tower.
Athens – TEAM 2: If you go to Athens, you'll (be able to) see the Parthenon.
Each team receives two points for a correct sentence. They lose one point for a grammatical error and one point for a factual error.

Activity Book Key

Exercise 1

1. If it rains, we'll stay in the car.
2. If it's cold, we'll go to a café.
3. If the beach is crowded, we'll go to another beach.
4. If all the beaches are crowded, we'll go to a park.
5. If the parks are closed, we'll come home.

Exercise 2

1. He's buying four.
2. He'll pay £9.94 altogether.
3. If he doesn't like them, he'll return them (within ten days).
4. He'll have to pay nothing./He won't have to pay anything.
5. No, he won't.
6. He'll have to buy at least six records in the first year.

Exercise 3

Numbers 2., 3., and 4. are correct.
Numbers 1., 5., and 6. are incorrect.

CORRECTED SENTENCES:
1. They'll get there fast if they go by train.
5. If you eat that ice-lolly, you'll feel ill.
6. It'll switch on if you press that button.

If you don't find them . . .

Language use	Ask about and state consequences
Grammar	First conditional: *What will happen if I shoot the creatures?* *If you don't look behind the satellite door, you won't find the sword.*
Vocabulary	bottom crash captain escape creature explode enemy fight instruction float manual shoot laser gun digital planet flesh-eating satellite on fire SOS everywhere capture

Materials

The numbers 1 to 9 folded up in a hat or other receptacle.

Text and Exercise 1

Introduce the theme by asking the students if they like science fiction and what science fiction book or film they have most enjoyed. As individual students describe their favourite to the class, provide them with any vocabulary that they need. With books open, students look at the picture and tell you what they think is happening. Use the picture to pre-teach some of the important vocabulary, e.g: *spaceship*, *planet*, *creature*. Students read the first paragraph and find out what the situation is. They should try to guess the meaning of any unknown vocabulary and, if necessary, check it in their dictionaries. Students then discuss the answers to Exercise 1 in pairs.

Exercise 2

Ask students to read the instructions in the second paragraph of the text, under the heading *How to play the game*. Explain any unknown vocabulary. Have the numbers 1 to 9 ready in a hat, cup or box so that you can demonstrate the game. Draw students' attention to the box with the *Key to the numbers* in it. Take a number out of the hat, ask two students to form the relevant question and answer from the box and practise them. Refer students back to the example in the instructions if necessary. Put students into pairs and ask each pair to write out the numbers 1–9 on nine pieces of paper and to put them in a container or place them face down on the desk. Each student should read only half the key. Student A looks at the 'Instruction' column and covers up the 'What will happen' column and

Student B does the opposite. Student A picks up one number at a time and asks Student B the relevant question from the 'Instruction' column. Student B replies. The game finishes when they have 'found' the sword, the laser gun and the manual. Alternatively, the students can play simultaneously in their pairs. They both pick out their own sequence of numbers and play alternately. The first person to have 'found' the sword, the laser gun and the manual wins.

Exercise 3

Ask students to read the example sentence in the Look! box. Check their understanding. Point out that the two clauses in a first conditional sentence can be both positive, both negative, or there can be one positive clause and one negative clause. Remind them that *will not* contracts to *won't*.

Students then complete the sentences in Exercise 3 and write them in their notebooks.

Exercise 4

Students complete the sentences and compare them in pairs. Some variation in the choice of language is possible.

 Oral exercises 3 and 4

Extra activities

1. Draw a horrible creature

Set up a competition to see which student can create the worst creature. Ask the students to draw and write a description of the most horrible creature they can imagine. They can do this alone or in pairs. When they have finished, they pass around their drawings and descriptions for each other to look at. The teacher then judges the contest.

2. The first conditional creature

Tell the students that they have landed on a planet and found some strange creatures (e.g. those they drew in Activity 1). The creatures are very friendly, although they look horrible. They speak English but they can only use first conditional sentences. As visitors to the creatures' planet, the students have many questions to ask the creatures. Put the students into teams and give them a few minutes to plan five questions to ask the creatures. They can use any structure in their questions, but they cannot ask any questions about the past. The teams then take it in turns to ask each other the questions. The other team must reply using the first conditional. A point is given for each correct reply in the first conditional, e.g:

s1: Where do we go to sleep?
s2: If you go to spaceship Number 3, you'll find some beds there.
s1: Is there food on this planet?
s2: If you come with us, we'll give you some food.

Activity Book Key

Exercise 1

1. If I pass my exams, I'll have a party.
2. I won't have a party if I don't pass my exams.
3. If you train harder, you'll be in the team.
4. I'll tell Miss Harris if you don't give me my book back.
5. I won't say anything if you don't want me to.
6. Your dad will be angry if you get home late.
7. If you write to me, I'll write to you.
8. If he doesn't come, he won't play in our team.

Exercise 2

1. a) If it rains, I'll go to the cinema with Mary.
   b) If it doesn't rain, I'll play tennis with Mary.
2. a) If it's cold, I'll go to the museum with Jack.
   b) If it isn't cold, I'll go walking with Jack.
3. a) If it's sunny, I'll go to the beach.
   b) If it isn't sunny, I'll go shopping.
4. a) If it's windy, I'll go windsurfing.
   b) If it isn't windy, I'll go canoeing.

 Exercise 3

TAPESCRIPT
Look at your book and listen to the radio programme.
Write the problems and the suggested solutions.

CHORUS:	536 3655
KATIE KING:	We have a caller on Line One . . . er . . . Derek. Good morning, Derek. Do you have a problem for Dr Davies?
DEREK:	Er, yes. My problem is, I haven't been to my German class for a month because I was ill. Now it's too difficult, and I can't understand the lessons.
DR DAVIES:	Have you talked to your teacher about this?
DEREK:	No, I was too embarrassed.
DR DAVIES:	You'll have to talk to your teacher first, Derek. You won't solve your problem if you don't talk about it. So, talk it over with the people at school and see if they can help you.
KATIE KING:	OK, we have a caller on Line Four . . . Margaret.
MARGARET:	Good morning, Dr Davies.
DR DAVIES:	Hi.
MARGARET:	I'm an athlete, and I do a lot of running.
DR DAVIES:	Good.
MARGARET:	But I get very sore feet. What can I do about it?
DR DAVIES:	How far do you run?
MARGARET:	About ten kilometres a day.
DR DAVIES:	Where do you do your running?
MARGARET:	Oh the roads around my house.
DR DAVIES:	Hmm. I have two pieces of advice. First, run on grass if you can. It hurts your feet less. Second, run only three or four kilometres until your feet feel better. And if they don't get better, stop running and go to your doctor.
MARGARET:	OK, OK . . . thanks very much. Goodbye.
KATIE KING:	And our next caller is . . . Peter.
PETER:	Doctor, I have a question that I'm worried about. I play football, but I'm nearly thirty. Will I have to give it up soon?

DR DAVIES: Peter, some people play football when they're sixty. There's a professional footballer at the moment who's forty. The rule is, keep playing the sport until it becomes too much hard work. When it gets too difficult, then it's time to stop.

1. PROBLEM: Derek hasn't been to his German class. He was ill. Now it's too difficult.
   SOLUTION: Talk to his teacher.
2. PROBLEM: Margaret gets sore feet when she runs.
   SOLUTION: Run on grass. Run only three or four kilometres. Go to a doctor if they don't get better.
3. PROBLEM: Peter plays football, but he's nearly thirty. Is he too old?
   SOLUTION: It's not really a problem. Keep playing until it gets too difficult, then stop.

You must run faster.

Language use	Give advice

Grammar	Modal verb *must*;
	Comparative of adverbs with *-er*:
	You must run faster.
	Comparative of adverbs with
	  more:
	You must train more regularly.
	First conditional (revision):
	*If you don't train harder, you won't
	  get in the team.*

Vocabulary	fit criticise performance praise superstar train annoy sensible behave regularly

Materials
A picture of someone who could be a college student.

Background notes
fifteen miles (See Exercise 3.) Approximately 24 kilometres.

Presentation
Show the students a picture of someone who could be a college student. Introduce the character e.g. *This is Mike.* Tell the class that he has just finished his last year at college. He enjoyed college very much but he did not work very hard and unfortunately he failed his exams. Build up a picture of his life at college and elicit as much as possible from the students about how they think he spent his time. Make it clear that he had a good time and did not work much, e.g: *He went to a lot of parties, He always went to bed late, He didn't go to all his classes.* Then tell the students that he has failed his exams but he has the chance to take them again. He very much wants to pass them this time and he goes to see his tutor (or teacher). Ask the class what they think the tutor says to him and lead into an introduction of *must* and of comparative adverbs. (*Must* may be revision for the students as it was introduced in Students' Book 2.)

 Introduce an example of *must* with a comparative adverb. Explain that Mike's tutor wants him to work hard this time and she knows he did not work very hard last time. Students repeat a model sentence: *You must work harder.* Introduce and drill a model sentence using a comparative adverb with *more*, e.g: *You must come to classes more regularly.* Point out to students that one-syllable adverbs, e.g: *hard* and *fast*, and the adverb *early* add *-er* to become comparative but that adverbs of two or more syllables are preceded by *more* to become comparative. The comparative of *well* is *better*.

Go on to elicit and practise other example sentences. Prompt the students if necessary, e.g:
  T: bed late
  S: You must go to bed earlier.
  T: homework
  S: You must do your homework more often.

 Note: Students may ask about the difference between *must* and *have to*. Explain in the L1 that we can generally use either but that *must* is used more often when the speaker imposes the obligation, e.g. Trainer to sportsperson: *You must train harder*, and *have to* is used more often when the obligation comes from the situation or from another person and not from the speaker, e.g: *We have to wear school uniform.* It is often associated with routines, e.g: *I have to get up early in the mornings.* Also, *must* does not have different tense forms, so *have to* is used when we need a different tense, such as the past tense.

🔲 Read and listen
With books closed, introduce the theme. Teach *fit*. Tell the students that you want to be fit and you want to be good at a particular sport. Ask them what you must do. Revise *to train* and *training*. Tell the students they are going to hear about Kirsty who runs for a club. Write some focus questions on the board: *What is Kirsty's problem? What does she do about it? What happens in the end?*

 Play the tape with books closed and then check students' answers to the focus questions. The students then listen again with their books open.

Exercise 1
The students do this alone and then compare their answers in pairs. Answer any vocabulary questions when you check through the answers.

KEY
1. Picture 4   2. Picture 5   3. Picture 2   4. Pictures 6 and 7
5. Picture 3   6. Picture 1

Exercise 2
Build up an oral summary with the students first. Ask them to put the story into the past tense and help them to fill out the details and link the events. Students should think about the story behind the speech lines and imagine what is going on.

MODEL ANSWER
Kirsty is a runner in a club. Two months ago she was not running very well and her trainer, Gail, wasn't very pleased with her. Kirsty was in a race and before the race, Gail told her that she must/had to run faster. However, Kirsty lost the race and Gail was annoyed with her and criticised her. So Kirsty decided to train hard. She trained every day and night. Gail was pleased with her and praised her. In the next race, Kirsty came first and won a gold medal.

Exercise 3

Ask students to look at the task in their books and encourage them to discuss what the answers may be before they listen. Then play the tape straight through and ask the students if they were right. Students listen to the tape a second time and take notes. Stop the tape once or twice to give them the opportunity to do this.

TAPESCRIPT

Listen to a runner talking about his training. Look at your book and take notes.

INTERVIEWER: Now Alan, you're a runner. How much training do you do?

ALAN: Well, I try and train every day. That's . . . usually means I run every day. Sometimes I have short runs, sometimes long runs, but . . . er . . . when I'm in peak training I run every day.

INTERVIEWER: How would you say that your training has changed perhaps, say, over the last three years?

ALAN: Well, I certainly do longer runs now. I like to have one run each week of about fifteen miles. I find that that gives me a lot of strength and that's something I've been trying to develop over the last couple of years. It helps you obviously in longer races, but it's surprising, but it also helps you in shorter races as well, particularly towards the end of those.

INTERVIEWER: Are there a lot of differences between training in the winter and training in the summer?

ALAN: Generally, yes. In the winter, the weather and the dark evenings prevent you from doing certain types of training. Consequently you tend to run for longer distances at a slower pace, probably around the roads. Um . . . during the summer, you're able to do different types of training and as the weather becomes warmer, you tend to want to run faster and you'll train on the shorter distances at a faster pace.

Exercise 4

Ask the students to read the example sentences in the Look! box and see if they remember the rule. Answer any questions the students have on vocabulary in the exercise. The students then do the exercise on their own or in pairs. Tell students that the *if* clauses are all negative.

Exercise 5

Discuss with the class what an article about running should include. Ask them to refer back to their notes from the listening exercise and to add any additional suggestions. Play the tape from Exercise 3 again if necessary. Ask for ideas for a title for the article. Then find out which sports the students want to

write about and put them into groups accordingly, i.e. all the students who want to write about running should work together. The students discuss the article in their groups and write it together or individually. The groups can then exchange articles and read each other's.

 Oral exercise 5

Extra activities

1. Match the sentences

Write out a list of problems with responses using *You must . . .*, e.g: *I feel tired all the time. You must go to bed earlier.* Put students into groups. Give each group a number of problems and replies on separate pieces of paper and ask them to match them together.

2. Adverb comparison bingo

Ask students to draw nine boxes on a piece of paper to make a bingo card. Write a list of about twenty comparative adverbs on the board, e.g: *harder, better, more quickly.* Students fill in all nine of their bingo card boxes, choosing from the list of twenty on the board. Rub out the list. Say the adverbs (not in their comparative form) in random order and at a fast pace. Students cross out the corresponding comparative form on their cards. The first student to cross out all their comparative adverbs shouts *Bingo* and is the winner.

Activity Book Key

Exercise 1
1. B   2. C   3. D   4. A

Exercise 2
c) best   b) strong   c) smart   a) faster than
b) harder than   c) more regularly

Exercise 3
Open exercise

Exercise 4
TROUBLE

LESSON 29 Stargazing

Language use	Make comparisons
	Give instructions
Grammar	Quantifiers *all, some, other/others, many, every*:
	All stars have different colours.
	Every star has a different colour.
	Many stars have a temperature of over 1,000°C.
Vocabulary	archer ram
	astronomer reptile
	atom scorpion
	balance soil
	bull star
	cloud temperature
	constellation virgin
	crab water carrier
	dense zodiac
	dwarf depend
	galaxy gaze
	giant vary
	goat brightly
	hydrogen gas dim
	pattern closely
	plough

Background notes

The signs of the zodiac These are also sometimes called 'star signs' or 'birth signs'. Our sign is dependent on the date of our birth. Each sign is associated with certain characteristics and the people born under this sign are all supposed to have these characteristics, e.g. Leos are said to be leaders.

Picture

Ask the students to try to find their star sign in the picture. If the students are familiar with star signs, put them into groups to discuss what they know about the characteristics of each sign. If they are interested in the topic, extend the discussion. Ask them if they think they have the characteristics of their sign and if they make friends more easily with people of any particular sign.

Read and answer

In small groups, students discuss the answers to the three questions before they read the text. One person from each group then reports back to the class. Encourage the students to discuss what they are not sure about. The students then read the text to find out if they were correct and answer the questions in their groups. Ask them to look up in

their dictionaries any new vocabulary which they need to know in order to answer the questions. Check the answers with the class.

Text: The colours of stars

Ask: *What colour is a star? Are they all the same colour? Are they all the same size?* Students read the text to check their answers.

Exercise 2

Ask students to read the exercise and check that they understand the vocabulary. They may need to refer back to the text to write the questions.

KEY
1. What is a constellation?
2. Where does the word 'zodiac' come from?
3. What does the colour of stars depend on?/What colour are stars?
4. What colour are the hottest stars?
5. Do all stars live for the same length of time?
6. What is a galaxy?

Presentation

Direct students to the Look! box. Point out, in the L1 if necessary, that:
- *all, many, some* and *other* (as quantifiers) are followed by a plural noun (where the noun is countable)
- *every* is followed by a singular noun
- *others* is a pronoun and can replace *other* + plural noun when the noun has already been referred to.

Drill an example sentence, chorally and individually, and substitute the different quantifiers, as follows:
T: Listen and repeat: 'All stars have different colours.'
S: All stars have different colours.
T: Many.
S: Many stars have different colours.
T: Every.
S: Every star has a different colour.
etc.

Exercise 4

After the group discussion, discuss the answers with the whole class:
1. False. Some cannot, e.g. ostrich, emu, penguin.
2. True.
3. False. Some snakes do not.
4. False. Some do not, e.g. pines and conifers.
5. False. Some rivers flow into other rivers, lakes or deserts.
6. False. Some plants live in water.

Extra activities

1. Noughts and crosses

Draw this grid on the board:

a few	every	other
many	others	all
a lot of	some	not many

Divide the class into a noughts team and a crosses team. Each team takes it in turns to produce a sentence using one of the words in the grid. If the sentence is correct, rub out the word in the grid and put in a nought or a cross, as appropriate. The aim of the game is to get a row of three noughts or crosses in any direction, horizontally, vertically or diagonally. The first team to do this is the winner.

2. Project: Stargazing

Draw a diagram of The Plough constellation on the board and ask the students to copy it into their project books:

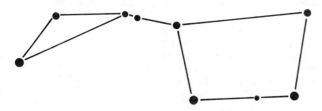

Ask them to watch the stars on a clear night and see if they can see The Plough. They should then record the event next to the diagram in their project books and report it to the class. Ask them to note down when they saw it and where they were.

Activity Book Key

Exercise 1
1. All stars have
2. Every student has to
3. Most people have
4. Some animals don't
5. Many schools are
6. Other people agree

Exercise 2
Open exercise

Exercise 3
We asked a scientist: 'Does the earth move round the sun very quickly or not?' Her name is Doctor Mackenzie and she works at a university in Italy. She said: 'The earth goes round the sun more quickly than some planets and more slowly than others. The question is a difficult one to answer because the answer depends on what you mean when you say "very quickly".'

Exercise 4
The largest planet is Jupiter.
The order of planets from the sun is: Mercury, Venus, Earth, Mars, Jupiter, Saturn, Uranus, Neptune, Pluto.

Vocabulary	finger	develop
	palm	indicate
	palmistry	even-tempered
	personality	methodical
	shape	nervous
	talent	talented
	texture	
Speechwork	Pronunciation: /tʃ/ capture	
	Stress: didida da dadi, If you DON'T RUN FASTer	
	Intonation:	
	If you 'don't 'train harder,/ you 'won't 'win the match.	

Background notes

A phone-in A popular type of radio programme where an expert or famous person is brought into the studio to answer listeners' questions on the phone.

Read

Teach: *palm, palm reading, palmist, palmistry*. Ask the class questions to introduce the theme: *Have you ever had your palms read? When? Where? What did the palmist say? What do you think of palmistry?*

Teach and practise the vocabulary in the text which describes characteristics, e.g: *talented, even-tempered*, etc. Write a focus question on the board: *How does a palmist read your hand?* Students read the passage and answer the focus question.

Answer

Give students time to look at the questions in the Students' Book and check that they understand the vocabulary. Ask them to read the text again, to discuss the answers to the questions in pairs and to look up in their dictionaries any vocabulary which they need to answer the questions.

Note: In the text there are examples of the first conditional and also of conditional sentences which have a present tense in both clauses, e.g. *If you have a strong Heart Line, you are warm and loving*. If you wish to point this out to the students, tell them that this type of conditional sentence refers to things which are always true, e.g. scientific facts.

Word study

With the students' help, write the adjectives from the text on the board. Check that the students understand all the words. The students then put them into two columns as instructed in the Students' Book.

- Put students into pairs to read each other's palms, using their lists. They then compare the palm reading with their own assessment of themselves

and discuss whether they agree with the analyses. Finally, they report back to the class. Encourage the class to discuss their opinions of palmistry.

Listen

Check that students understand what a phone-in programme is and find out what they think of such programmes. Ask them what kind of problems they would expect people to discuss on a 'problem phone-in'. Students then read the questions in the Students' Book. Explain *has no future* (Question 3). Play the tape, then check through the answers with the class. Ask the students what they think Ben should do.

TAPESCRIPT

Listen to Ben on 'Problem Phone-in'. Look at your book and answer True or False.

ANNA: . . . And don't forget Karen, you can send for our information sheet. Right, our next caller on the line is Ben. Are you there, Ben?

BEN: Yeah.

ANNA: What can we do for you, Ben?

BEN: Well, I've been unemployed for over six months.

ANNA: So have three million others!

BEN: Yeah, but I've just found a job as a packer . . . er . . . in a biscuit factory.

ANNA: And it's boring!

BEN: No, it's not. I like it actually. But it won't get me anywhere, will it? In the future. Know what I mean? I'd rather go to college.

ANNA: Is that your problem?

BEN: No. You see, I live at home with my mother, who's ill. She can't work and she's on Social Security.

ANNA: Do you give her any money?

BEN: Sure I do. That's the point. She really needs my money for medicines and things.

ANNA: Are you the only other person at home?

BEN: Yeah, and well, I applied for a place on an engineering course at the local college.

ANNA: And?

BEN: I've got a place starting next September.

ANNA: But that's just great Ben. Aren't you pleased?

BEN: Yeah, I really want to go but . . .

ANNA: But your mother doesn't want you to?

BEN: No, my mother does want me to but I don't know how my mother will manage without my money. If I go to college, I won't be able to pay her anything.

ANNA: What do you think listeners? Our Hot Line is open to receive your calls on 01 01 . . .

Write

Ask the students to tell you what Ben's problem is and what choices are possible. If necessary, play the tape again. Prompt the students into using a first conditional structure, e.g: *If he goes to college, he won't be able to give his mother any money*. The students then write the letter, referring back to the true/false questions to help them. Point out that there is no 'correct' letter; they can write it in different ways.

MODEL ANSWER

(Ben's address)

(Date)

Dear Helpline,

   My problem is this: I have been unemployed for six months but I have just found a job in a biscuit factory. I like it but it has no future and I'd rather go to college. I've got a place at the local college starting next September. I want to go but my mother is ill and can't go to work. I give her money to help her. If I go to college, I won't be able to pay her anything, but if I don't go to college, I won't be able to get a better job. My mother wants me to go to college but I think she needs my money. What do you think I should do?

Yours sincerely,

Ben Turner

Dictionary skills
n. (noun)
palmistry /ˈpɒːmə̩stri/
the art or practice of a palmist
(from the Longman Dictionary of Contemporary English)
Note: If students are using a bi-lingual dictionary, they can write in a translation of the word *palmistry*. If using the LDOCE or the Longman Active Study Dictionary, point out to students that small capitals are used for cross-references. The definition is not repeated for each word in the word family. The student should therefore look at the definition of *palmist* to understand *palmistry*.

   Point out that when two symbols are given for one sound, e.g: /ə̩/, it means that the word is commonly pronounced in both ways.

Grammar summary
Remind students that:
- in the first conditional, the *if* clause is in the present simple and the main clause is in the simple future
- the *if* clause can come first or second
- one-syllable adverbs add *-er* to form the comparative
- adverbs ending in *-ly* are preceded by *more* to form the comparative (except *early*)
- *every* is followed by a singular noun
- *all*, *some* and *many* are followed by plural nouns (if the noun is countable).

Extra activities

1. Roleplay: Problem phone-in
All the students think of a problem for the phone-in, real or imaginary. Working in twos or threes they take it in turns to phone up with their problem and the other student or students ask questions and offer advice.

2. What's important to you?
The students first work on their own to put the following list into order of priority.

   They then form pairs or groups and compare their lists and try to agree on a final order. The class may add to the list any further ideas of their own before they start.

health	children
money	power/fame
an interesting job	good looks
love	intelligence
a good social life	

Activity Book Key

Exercise 1
1. If you don't come home early, you won't do your homework properly.
2. If you don't do your homework properly, you won't pass your exams.
3. If you don't pass your exams, you won't go to college.
4. If you don't go to college, you won't get a good job.
5. If you don't get a good job, you won't have any money.
6. If you don't have any money, you won't be very happy.

Exercise 2
Tina is a clever girl but she is rather lazy. She must work harder in class. We are also worried about her homework. She doesn't take enough time to do it. If she wants to pass her exams, she will have to do her homework more carefully. Her class teacher says Tina is often rather silly in class, and she'd better behave more sensibly.

   On the other hand, she plays football and tennis much more regularly than last year and she runs faster than any other student her age. If she puts as much energy into her work as her sport, she will become a perfect student.

Exercise 3
1. All   2. Many   3. others   4. Many   5. is
6. most

Exercise 4
catch / miss, pull / push, cruel / kind, ask / answer, dark / light

Exercise 5
To get the most number of points, Andy should go to the satellite on A2, then to the plastic planet on A1. After that, he should go to the satellite on B1 and the plastic planet on C1. Finally he should go to the spaceship on C2.
(Total points: 250)

Exercise 6
Open exercise

 Speechwork Lessons 26–30

Pronunciation
Listen and repeat.
/tʃ/ /tʃ/ /tʃ/ capture creature picture

Listen and repeat.
We captured the creature!

Stress
Listen and repeat.
didida da dadi, didida da dadi, didida da dadi
If you DON'T RUN FASTer,
If you DON'T MOVE QUICKer,
If you DON'T TRAIN HARDer

Intonation
Listen and repeat.

If you 'don't 'train harder,/you 'won't 'win
the match.

If you 'don't 'work harder,/you 'won't 'pass
the test.

If you 'don't 'run faster,/you 'won't 'catch
the bus.

Language use	Talk about obligations
	Invite, refuse and give excuses
Grammar	Verb *have got* + infinitive with *to* (obligation):
	I've got to go on a survival course.
	Reflexive pronouns *myself*, etc:
	We've got to build *ourselves* a shelter.
Vocabulary	barbecue — amuse
	detail — cheer up
	gala — confirm
	gran — occupy
	granny — depressed
	mirror — survival
	patience — yourself/ves
	shelter — Don't worry.
	skill
	tent
	violin

Picture

Ask the students questions about the picture to introduce the camping theme and some of the vocabulary from the dialogue, e.g: *Where are they? What are they sleeping in? Have you ever been camping? Do you know how to put up a tent? What can you build a shelter from? When you're camping, how do you cook?*

 Dialogue

Write a focus question on the board: *Why can't Andy and Kate go to Auntie Megan's party?* Play the tape and check the answer to the question. See if the students can deduce the meaning of any vocabulary that was not pre-taught, e.g. *survival course, out of doors* and *Don't worry*, if not, explain. Explain *Gran* and *Granny*.

Exercise 1

The students read Exercise 1, listen to the tape again and then copy and complete the notice. Ask them what they think a *skill* is and check that they understand the rest of the vocabulary in the exercise before they start.

KEY
The Youth Survival Course teaches young people how to *look after themselves out of doors*. The course includes training in the following skills:
How to:
1. *build a shelter*
2. *put up a tent*
3. *make a fire*
4. *cook their own food.*
Please contact Penny Gardener for more details.

Presentation

Play the first few lines of the dialogue again and ask the students to listen to the way that Andy and Kate reply to Granny's question. Stop the tape after *I've got to go on a survival course with the school.* Clarify the meaning of *have got to* and check students' understanding. Ask students to study the example sentence in the first Look! box. Highlight the form:
- *have got* is followed by the infinitive with *to*
- in the third person singular it is *has got to*
- the contractions *'ve* and *'s* are used, e.g: *They've got to . . .*, *She's got to . . .*

The students listen to the dialogue again and repeat.

Note: *Have got to* is used in a similar way to *have to* to express obligation. It is used most of all in informal conversation. For single actions, both *have to* and *have got to* are correct, e.g: *I've got to go now* or *I have to go now.* For repeated or habitual actions, *have to* is the correct form, e.g: *Do you have to wear a uniform?*

Exercise 2

Students read the example exchange. Check their understanding of it and then drill it. One half of the class takes the part of A and the other the part of B, then they change parts. Explain any unknown vocabulary in the exercise. Put the students into pairs to make conversations.

[cassette icon] **Exercise 3**

Ask a few of the students to tell you about the last time they could not come to school and what the reason was. Students copy the chart. Explain *attend* and point out to the students that they must find out what event the pupils cannot attend. The students listen to the tape and, in pairs, complete the information in the chart. Play the tape again for them to check. Stop at the examples of *have got to* and ask the students to repeat the sentence. Check the information with the class. Students can then roleplay the conversations between the school secretary and the two teachers (Miss Brown and Mrs Shepherd) when she gives them the message.

TAPESCRIPT
Listen to these parents telephoning the school secretary. Look at your book and copy and complete the chart.

1.
SECRETARY: Morning. Bedford School, school secretary speaking.
MRS FOSTER: Oh, oh, good morning, this is Billy Foster's mother. Billy Foster who's in Class 2C. Miss Brown is his teacher.
SECRETARY: Good morning, Mrs Foster. What can I do for you?
MRS FOSTER: It's about Billy. He's ill. He's seen the doctor. The doctor says it's flu and he's got to stay in bed.

SECRETARY: I'm sorry to hear that. I'll tell Miss Brown.
MRS FOSTER: He's singing in the school concert this evening but I'm afraid he can't be there.
SECRETARY: Don't worry Mrs Foster. I'll tell Miss Brown that Billy is ill with flu and won't be there this evening.
MRS FOSTER: Thank you so much. Billy's really disappointed that he can't come.
SECRETARY: I'm sure he is. Thanks for calling Mrs Foster. Bye.
MRS FOSTER: Bye.

2.
SECRETARY: Morning, Bedford School. This is the Head's secretary.
MR PARKS: Oh, good morning. This is Mr Parks. I'm Jenny Parks's father.
SECRETARY: Jenny Parks. She's in Class 3B, isn't she?
MR PARKS: That's right. Well, I'm afraid she can't go on the school trip tomorrow.
SECRETARY: Oh, you mean the trip to the zoo?
MR PARKS: Yes. She can't go because she's got to go to London for a music exam.
SECRETARY: I see. Right. I'll make a note of that to tell Mrs Shepherd. Jenny Parks, Class 3B, cannot go on the school outing to the zoo tomorrow because she's got to go to London for a music exam.
MR PARKS: Exactly. Thanks.
SECRETARY: Not at all. Thank you for letting us know. Goodbye.

Exercise 4

MODEL ANSWER

Dear Mrs Shepherd,

This is just to confirm that Billy cannot sing in the school concert this evening because he's ill with flu and he's got to stay in bed. He's very sorry that he cannot come.

Yours sincerely,

Mrs. J. Foster

Exercise 5

Give the students a few minutes to read the personal quiz on their own and then explain any new vocabulary. Ask the students to pick out the reflexive in each question and point out that reflexives are used here because the subject and the object or indirect object of the action are the same. Direct students to the second Look! box and point out that singular reflexives end with *self* and the plural ones end with *selves*.

Ask the students a few of the questions in the quiz to provide example dialogues and then get the students to complete the questionnaire in pairs. Put the pairs into groups of four and ask each student to report on their partner's answers to the other pair.

🔲 *Oral exercise 1*

Extra activities

1. A survival package
Tell the students that they are going to spend a week in a remote area. (If possible, give them the name of somewhere in their country.) There will be no shops nearby and they will have no transport to travel to the nearest town. They can take with them only six items from the following list: sleeping bag, rope, matches, cooking pots, tent, blankets, fresh water, tinned food, camping gas stove, torch, mirror, books, first aid kit, knife, fishing rod, two-way radio, extra clothes, toiletries (soap, flannel, toothpaste, toothbrush, towel), hairbrush. The class may add to this list if they have any further ideas before the discussion starts.

The students, in pairs, must agree on a list of the six items they will take. The pairs then join together into groups of four to six and again try to agree on a list. Finally, all the groups compare their lists.

The discussion should incorporate use of the first conditional, and modals (*should, must, have got to, have to, may*), e.g: *We've got to take a tent. Where will we sleep if we don't take a tent? If we take a fishing rod, we'll be able to catch fish. I think we should/must/'ve got to/have to take some blankets*, etc.

2. Game: making excuses
Ask the students if they are coming to an event (real or imaginary), e.g: *Are you coming to my extra lesson on Saturday?* Go round the class asking all the students. They must answer straightaway with: *No, I'm afraid I can't* and an excuse that has not yet been used. If they cannot think of an excuse immediately or if they repeat an excuse, they are 'out'. When you get to the end of the class, go round again excluding the students who are out. The last student left in is the winner. When you have played the game once with the whole class, the students can play the game again in groups, and take it in turns to ask the question.

Activity Book Key

Exercise 1
1. Sorry, Lizzie. I've got to put up the tents.
2. I'm afraid she's got to put up the food tent.
3. No. They've got to cook (the) dinner.
4. Yes, she is. She's got to clean the van.
5. But he's got to get the sleeping bags ready.
6. No, you won't! You've got to make a fire.

Exercise 2
Open exercise

Exercise 3
After Ron and Margaret left the camp, the boys had to look after themselves. They were rather bored, so they decided to amuse themselves by making a fire. Mark burned himself with a match and then Peter cut himself with his penknife. Patrick was beginning to feel rather miserable now, so they decided to cheer themselves up by playing football. After a while, they were feeling better. 'This is great!' said Mark, 'I'm really enjoying myself now!' Then he tripped over the football and fell into the river.

Exercise 4
Open exercise

Ever since November . . .

Language use	Ask and talk about continuing actions
Grammar	Present perfect continuous with *how long, for* and *since*: *How long have you been living here?* *I've been living here since November/ for three weeks.*
Vocabulary	bamboo manage coconut rescue desert island row fishing rod tour lagoon shipwrecked pipe single-handed plenty ever since shell fortunately storm thirst

Background notes
(See Exercise 4)

to tour/to be on tour	To travel around giving concerts.
sell-out concert	All the tickets were sold.
lead singer	The main singer.
number 97 in the top 100	This refers to the top 100 of the hit parade.
hit parade	The 100 best-selling records. A new hit parade is compiled every week in Britain. Number 1 is the record which sold the most in the previous week.
new wave	A new style of music that started in the 1980s.

Presentation
Tell the students that you are going to talk about yourself for a minute. Include information which can be used to lead into examples of the present perfect continuous with *for* or *since*, e.g: *I went to (Bristol University), where I studied (English) and (education). I left there in (1977) and started teaching at a school in (Bristol). I came to this school in (1983). I live in a (house) in (Islington) with (my husband). We moved there in (1985). I learnt to drive (last year) and bought a (second-hand Fiat). I now come to school by car.*

   Ask the students questions to check that they have understood what you have said. Give the information again, pausing to elicit or provide example sentences in the present perfect continuous. Clarify the concept of the present perfect continuous, e.g: *I started teaching in (1977), (eleven) years ago, and I'm still teaching now. I've been teaching for (eleven years). I've been teaching since (1977).* Get students to repeat the example sentences.

Elicit or provide further example sentences arising from the information you gave the students about yourself, e.g: *I've been teaching at this school for (five years)/since (1983). I've been living in a (house) in (Islington) for (three years)/since (1985). I've been driving a Fiat for (a/one year)/since (last year).*

   Draw a time line on the board to illustrate the meaning:

I've been teaching for eleven years.		
	PAST	PRESENT FUTURE
I started teaching in 1977.		I am still teaching now.

Elicit or demonstrate a question with *How long . . . ?* Write an example on the board: *How long have you been teaching? I've been teaching for ten years.*

   The students can then write five positive sentences about themselves using the present perfect continuous with *for* or *since*.

Picture
Ask questions about the picture to establish the situation and introduce some of the vocabulary. e.g: *This is Des. Where is he? Why do you think he's there? What happened to him? Why do you think he was shipwrecked? What does the picture tell you about how he has lived on the island?* Give students the vocabulary that you cannot elicit from them. Do not worry about the structures that the students use at this stage.

Diary
Ask the students to read Des's diary and to note down three things he has done since he came to the island. (He has cut down palm leaves, made a shelter, made a fishing rod, caught some fish, made a bamboo pipe, found some shells.) The students should use their dictionaries if necessary. Check their answers and explain any unknown vocabulary. Ask them to find the example of the present perfect continuous in the diary. (*I've been living on this island for three weeks.*)

Text

Write a focus question on the board: *Who wants to read Des's diary and why?* The students then read the introductory paragraph. Check their answers to the focus question and ask them what they think the new vocabulary in the text means, e.g: *to row, single-handed*, etc. Explain the vocabulary as necessary. Ask students to find the example of the present perfect continuous. (*He . . . has been living there ever since.*) Point out that *ever since* means since that time and suggests that it is quite a long time.

Exercise 1

Use the instructions to elicit the roleplay from the class. Remind students that the conversation takes place in the middle of December. Refer students to the Look! box for a model question and answers. Practise the dialogue chorally with one half of the class as Des and the other half as the captain and then change roles. Put the students into pairs to roleplay the conversation, e.g:

CAPTAIN: How long have you been living here?
DES: For a month.

Point out to the students that only the first answer requires *for* or *since*, and that when the captain asks, *Where have you been sleeping?*, we understand that he means: *Where have you been sleeping for the last month/ since you arrived on the island?* so it is not necessary for him to use *for* or *since* in the question.

Exercise 3

Remind students of the presentation when you told them about yourself. See how much they can remember and tell them to ask you a question to check any information they are not sure of, using *How long have you . . . ?* Then ask the students to look at the exercise and build up a model dialogue between two students with the rest of the class listening. Put students into pairs to ask each other the questions.

🔲 Exercise 4

Students read the task in Exercise 4. Check that they understand it and play the tape. The students then take notes and compare their answers in pairs. Play the tape again if necessary. After checking the answers with the class, ask the students to produce a complete sentence for each answer, e.g: *They've been touring for six months.*

TAPESCRIPT
Listen to an interview with a rock band on tour. Look at your book and answer the questions.

ANNOUNCER: And now a report from Mandy Maxwell on tour with one of Britain's brightest new bands: Black Magic.

MANDY: From the dark streets of Newcastle to the smart clubs of Long Beach, California, this band has come a long way. I managed to catch them at the end of their six-month European tour, immediately after their sell-out concert at the Odeon, Hammersmith. I talked to Carl Derry, lead singer of Black Magic.

MANDY: Great concert, Carl, just great.

CARL: Thanks.

MANDY: I understand you're just finishing your European tour.

CARL: Yeah, er, we've been touring for six months. It's been a long time.

MANDY: How do you all get on together?

CARL: Er, pretty well. You have to when you're touring.

MANDY: How long have you been playing together as a band?

CARL: Well, Ray and I used to be with a band called The Bellboys. Then we met the others. We started playing together in a club called the Hungry Horse in Newcastle, and that was in June 1986. So we've been together . . . Well, you work it out.

MANDY: What was your first record?

CARL: 'World of Strangers'. That was January 1987. Er, it reached number 97 in the top 100. It was really new wave!

MANDY: Well, I liked it.

CARL: Well, you must be the only person in the world who did!

MANDY: There's one question I know all your fans would like to know.

CARL: What's that?

MANDY: How did the band get its name?

CARL: Ah! After my girlfriend's dog, actually.

MANDY: Girlfriend's dog! Charming!

CARL: Yes, she had a dog called 'Black Magic' and I said: 'That's a silly name for a dog but it's a great name for a band!' And that's how we got our name.

MANDY: And now Black Magic are riding high in the hit parade with their new song 'Better Believe Me'.

Exercise 5

Do the exercise orally first. Each student should then write a paragraph about their favourite band or about 'Black Magic'. Put some questions on the board to help the students but tell them that they do not need to follow these exactly, e.g: *How long have they been playing together? When did they make their first record and what was it called? Have they been on tour recently? What are they doing now? Where did the band's name come from? What's the name of their latest song? Is it doing well?*

Joke time!

Ask students what the joke is. Check that they understand that you *grow* vegetables and that the same verb *grow* is used in the expression *grow tired*, which means to become tired.

 Oral exercise 2

Extra activities

1. Team game

Put the students into teams and give each team a list of occupations, e.g: *teacher, painter, pilot, astronaut, racing driver, hairdresser, carpenter, chef*. A member of Team A asks Team B, *What do you do?* A member of Team B replies, using an occupation from the list, e.g: *I'm a pilot*. Team A must then ask Team B a question in the present perfect continuous, e.g: *How long have you been flying planes?* or *How long have you been working as a pilot?* Team B replies. Demonstrate the activity T–S before students play the game.

Award a point for each correct question in the present perfect continuous and each correct answer. Students may use long or short replies, e.g: *(I've been flying planes) for five years.*

2. Shipwrecked

Tell the students they have just been shipwrecked on an island and they do not know how long it will be before they are rescued. They have with them some matches, a pen, paper, a bottle, a knife and some rope. Put them into small groups to decide what they need to do to live on the island, e.g. find water, build a shelter. Ask them to put the tasks into order of priority. Elicit a few ideas from the whole class before you put the students into groups. At the end, one student from each group should report back to the class. The discussion should incorporate the modals *should, have to* and *have got to* and comparatives, e.g: *We must find some water very quickly. A shelter is more important than a fire.*

Activity Book Key

Exercise 1

1. Jack's been waiting for fifteen minutes.
   Mark's been waiting since three o'clock.
2. Max has been living here for six years.
   Max's grandmother's been living here since 1985.
3. Tim's been studying French for two years.
   Sandra's been studying French since 1986.
4. Peter's been working for half an hour.
   Judy's been working since five o'clock.

Exercise 2

1. He's been crying for fifteen minutes.
2. The record's finished.
3. I've been reading this book for weeks but I haven't finished it yet.
4. I've read this book already.
5. I've been cleaning my room for hours.
6. I've cleaned my room. It's finished now.

Exercise 3

1. She's a singer.
2. It's called 3D.
3. Four.
4. It's called 'Pick me up'.
5. Yes, it is.
6. It's called 'I need shelter'.
7. She's been singing with the band for two years.

Language use	Comprehension, summary and vocabulary skills
Grammar	Reported speech with *know, say, hope* and *think*: *He said (that) he couldn't continue.*
Vocabulary	act body companion courage death end expedition heart hope	noon sleeping bag snowstorm thought complete hope brave worse surely

Background notes

Literary extract The extract is taken from *Race to the South Pole* by Lewis Jones and Bernard Brett, Longman Structural Readers Stage 4. It is about Scott and Amundsen's contest with each other and their battle against the terrible storms and cold of the Antarctic, told through their own words.

Sherlock Holmes (AB) A famous fictional detective in the books of Sir Arthur Conan Doyle (1859–1930). Holmes had a brilliant mind and could work out the complete solution to a crime with very little information. His assistant was called Dr Watson.

Read and listen and Exercise 1

Ask the students if they have heard of Robert Scott or Titus Oates and what they know about them. Then ask them to read the introductory paragraph. Check their understanding of it and explain new vocabulary. Discuss the theme. Ask the students: *Why do you think people go on expeditions? Would you like to go on an expedition to the South Pole? What would you like about it? What wouldn't you like? Many people die on expeditions. Is it better to do this than to stay at home all your life and die of old age?*

With books closed, play the first sentence of the tape. Write on the board: *Things are getting worse. Why?* Ask the students to predict why things might be getting worse. Then play the rest of the tape and discuss the answer to the question.

Students read the questions in Exercise 1. Check that they understand the vocabulary in the questions. Play the tape again and ask the students to read the text as they listen. The students then discuss the answers to the questions in pairs.

Write on the board the new vocabulary that you

have not yet taught from the text, e.g: *noon, poor,* etc. Ask the students to guess the meaning of the vocabulary from the context and then to check it in their dictionaries. When they have finished, ask them for the definitions and clarify the meanings as necessary.

Note: *to meet the end* means to die, *poor Titus Oates* – the writer, Robert Scott, uses *poor* because he feels sorry for Oates.

Presentation

Direct students to the Look! box. Ask them how the second sentences, the sentences in reported speech, are different from the first sentences, which are in direct speech. Point out that:

- when the reporting verb, e.g: *say, know, hope, think*, is in the past, the reported sentence goes from present to past: *is* becomes *was* and *can* becomes *could*
- *I* becomes *he* or *she*, and *we* becomes *they* when the person who is reporting is not the person who said or thought the sentence
- *that* is optional after the reporting verb.

Exercise 2

Do the exercise orally first and then ask the students to write the sentences in their notebooks.

Exercise 3

Ask the students to write the summary as if it were Scott's diary (so that they know which pronouns to use). Do the first sentences orally with the whole class. Then ask the students to work on their own and write the summary in their notebooks. Tell them to refer back to Scott's diary if necessary. Ask a few students to read out their summaries at the end. Correct any mistakes.

 Oral exercise 3

Extra activities

1. Oates's diary

Elicit from the class ideas as to what Oates may have written on the last page of his diary and then ask the students to write it.

2. Moral dilemma

Tell the students that they are on an expedition. There are five people on the expedition and two of them are ill. A third one has a bad foot and is probably suffering from frostbite. She/He needs another pair of boots. If she/he doesn't get another pair, her/his foot will get worse. The people on the expedition think that they are near the end of their journey and that they may come to a village in two or three days, but they are not sure. They only have enough food for three people for two days. They are travelling on foot.

33

Put the students into groups to decide what to do. One student from each group should then report back to the class. The discussion should incorporate the modals *should, must, have (got) to,* and the first conditional, e.g: *We must find a village. If we leave them here, they will die.*

Activity Book Key

Exercise 1
1. Mr Evers said that it was time to start.
2. Miss Hardy thought that more people were coming.
3. Mr Dauling hoped that Mr Jones wasn't going to wait much longer.
4. Ms Greenhall said that no one else was coming.
5. Mr Taylor knew that more people were arriving.
6. Ms Evans hoped the meeting was going to start soon.

 Exercise 2

TAPESCRIPT
Look at your book. Listen to the conversation and write what Sherlock Holmes says to Dr Watson.

HOLMES: Now, Watson. I know six things about the Ghost Burglar. First, I know that someone is taking money from the bank.
WATSON: Well, that's obvious, Holmes, from what we've heard.
HOLMES: Yes, yes, we have to start at the beginning. Second, I know that three people work in the bank on Saturdays.
WATSON: Miss Jenkins, Mr Prior and Mrs Thorne.
HOLMES: Precisely. Third, I think that Miss Jenkins is worried about something.
WATSON: Why do you say that?
HOLMES: Because of her pencil, Watson, the way she bites her pencil. Fourth, we know there is only one door into the bank.
WATSON: Yes, we looked at that this morning.
HOLMES: Fifth, I know that Mr Prior doesn't have a key to the door.
WATSON: I didn't know that.
HOLMES: That's because you didn't listen, Watson. And sixth, I think that Mrs Thorne has the answer to the problem.
WATSON: Mrs Thorne? Why Mrs Thorne?
HOLMES: Come along, Watson. We can find out the answer together.

KEY
1. I know that someone is taking money from the bank.
2. I know that three people work in the bank on Saturdays.
3. I think that Miss Jenkins is worried about something.
4. We know there is only one door into the bank.
5. I know that Mr Prior doesn't have a key to the door.
6. I think that Mrs Thorne has the answer to the problem.

Exercise 3
Holmes told me six things about the Ghost Burglar. First, he knew that someone was taking money from the bank. Second, he knew that three people worked in the bank on Saturdays. Third, he thought that Miss Jenkins was worried about something. Fourth, we knew there was only one door into the bank. Fifth, he knew that Mr Prior didn't have a key to the door. Sixth, he thought that Mrs Thorne had the answer to the problem.

LESSON 34 A race across Alaska

Language use	Define people, places and things
Grammar	Defining relative clauses with *who* and *which*: Libby Riddles is the woman *who won the world's toughest race*. Alaska is a territory *which is situated in North America*. Prepositions of place: *along, through, around, among, below over, across, above*
Vocabulary	ankle · deserve · block · hug · blubber · hunt · bridge · protect · dog team · situate · edge · wrap · fridge · bitter · husky dog · punishing · hut · smelly · igloo · smoky · inhabitant · tough · pile · wild-eyed · skin · above · sled · across · snow · ahead · steel · among · surface · around · terrain · over · territory · through · trail

Background notes

Eskimo	A member of one of the Arctic peoples from North Canada, Greenland, Alaska or Eastern Siberia. They are also called 'the Inuit' and this is the name they use themselves.
Literary extract (AB)	This is taken from *A Farewell to Arms* by Ernest Hemingway, published by Penguin.

Picture

With books open, students look at the map and the picture. Ask them what they know about the Eskimos. Put them into small groups to note down everything they know and everything they are not sure about. One person from each group should then report back to the class and the class can exchange and discuss their knowledge.

Read and answer

The students read the questions and then the text and discuss the answers in pairs. Check the answers with the class. Ask them if the text has given them any information that they were not sure about in

their earlier discussion. If some of the students' queries remain unanswered, ask them to go to a library to find the answers. Put the students into groups to discuss the meaning of the unknown vocabulary. Ask them to use their dictionaries to check it.

Newspaper article

Draw the students' attention to the headline:
Across 1,000 miles of Alaskan wilderness
The woman who won the world's toughest race
Explain *wilderness* and *toughest* and check that the students understand the other vocabulary. Ask the students to predict from the headline what the article will be about.

Write these questions on the board: *What kind of race do you think it was? Why was it the world's toughest race? What sort of woman do you think Libby Riddles is?* Get answers from the students before they start reading, then ask them to read the passage and find the right answers. Tell the students that it is not important to understand every word in the article but if they need to find out the meaning of a word in order to answer the questions, they should use their dictionaries.

Presentation

Write examples of defining and non-defining relative clauses with *who* and *which* on the board, e.g. defining: *Andrew is the student who sits next to the door. An owl is a bird which comes out at night*; non-defining: *Our school is in Milan, which is in the north of Italy. Our English teacher is Mrs Jones, who teaches us for five hours a week.*

Point out that:
- *who* is the relative pronoun for a person (e.g: *the student*)
- *which* is the relative pronoun for a thing (e.g: *a bird*)
- the first two examples are defining relative clauses, i.e. they define which person or thing we are talking about. The main clause does not make complete sense without the defining relative clause
- the third and fourth examples are non-defining relative clauses. The main clause is complete without the relative clause. A non-defining relative clause provides extra information about the person or thing
- a non-defining relative clause is generally preceded by a comma
- no commas are used in defining relative clauses.

77

34

Exercise 1

Students refer back to the reading texts to find the information to complete the sentences. For Numbers 1 to 4 they will need to refer back to the first text and for Numbers 5 and 6 to the newspaper article. Do the exercise orally with the whole class first then ask them to write the sentences in their notebooks.

Presentation

Demonstrate the meaning of the prepositions *along, through, around, among, below, over, across, above* by acting out example sentences and then drill them, e.g: *I'm walking along a row of desks/the edge of the classroom. I'm walking through the door. I'm walking around the chair,* etc.

Then ask the students to think of similar sentences which use a preposition. Put students into groups and ask them to act out their sentences to each other without speaking. The other students say what the sentence is.

Note: *over* often indicates movement from one side of an object to the other, e.g: *over the bridge, over the houses.*

Exercise 2

The students read the sentences. Explain any unknown vocabulary to them. They then write the complete sentences in their notebooks.

Exercise 3

Check that the students understand the questions. They then discuss them in pairs or groups before a discussion with the whole class. Encourage the students to talk freely and do not correct them too much at this stage.

 Oral exercise 4

Extra activities

1. Picture dictation

Describe a picture to the students. The students should listen to the description once straight through and then draw it during the second reading. Pause after each sentence during the second reading to give them time to draw. Aim to incorporate some of the prepositions introduced in this lesson and other prepositions taught before this lesson. When you have completed the dictation, ask the students to compare their pictures and then to dictate the description back to you so that you can draw it on the board. You could begin like this: *There's a house in the middle of the picture. It has four windows, two upstairs and two downstairs, and a door. It has a garden all around it and at the bottom of the front garden there is a river,* etc.

2. An Eskimo's diary

Tell the students to imagine that they are Eskimos living in igloos. Ask them to write a diary of what they did yesterday. They must imagine what an Eskimo would do at every part of the day.

Activity Book Key

Exercise 1

1. through . . . over 2. across . . . along
3. among . . . above 4. around . . . below
5. through . . . over 6. around . . . above

Exercise 2

1. They caught it at Montreux.
2. They got off at Lausanne.
3. No, they couldn't.
4. It went between the lake and houses.
5. They stayed in a (medium-sized) hotel.
6. It was raining.
7. The nearest thing they could see from their window was a garden with a wall.
8. It was above the wall.
9. It was across the street.
10. He saw the rain falling in the garden fountain./The rain was falling into the fountain.

Vocabulary	archway	leader
	arrow	parade
	castle	river bank
	hill	wedding
	hut	
Speechwork	Pronunciation: /f/ self, /v/ selves	
	Stress: didida didida, I've been WORKing so HARD	
	Intonation: How 'long have they been working here?	

Activity

Ask the students to look at the map and read the instructions. Check that they understand all the vocabulary used. The pictures should clarify the meaning in most cases. Start the activity off with the whole class. Then put the students into pairs to do it on their own from the beginning. Check through the directions with the class at the end. A few variations in the choice of language are possible. Use your hands to demonstrate the prepositions if you need to correct the students, e.g. one hand *under* the other, two fingers walking *along* or *across* the other hand. Point out to the students that they may use some of the prepositions more than once.

Roleplay

Elicit a model roleplay from the class. Drill it with two halves of the class taking it in turns to play each part. Then put the students into pairs to practise the roleplay. Finally, the students write the dialogue in their notebooks.

 Listen

Introduce the topic by briefly asking the students what they would like to do when they leave school and if anyone is planning to study abroad. Tell them that they are going to hear an interview with Carol, who is studying modern dance.

Write a focus question on the board: *Do you think Carol enjoys what she is doing?* Play the tape once. Students answer the question. Then students read the questions in the Students' Book. Check that they understand the vocabulary in the questions. Play the tape a second time, pausing every so often to enable students to note down the answers. Play the tape again if necessary and check through the answers with the class.

TAPESCRIPT
Listen to this interview with Carol, who is studying modern dance. Look at your book and answer the questions.

INTERVIEWER: Why Madrid, Carol?
CAROL: You mean why am I studying modern dance in Madrid?

INTERVIEWER: Yes.
CAROL: Because of Luis Perez. He's just the best in the world.
INTERVIEWER: The best?
CAROL: Well, he's not just a dancer you know, he's a teacher, at the Madrid Centre for Modern Dance.
INTERVIEWER: And how long have you been at the centre?
CAROL: I've been studying there for just under a year. I'd like to stay for another three months, at least.
INTERVIEWER: Where are you from, Carol?
CAROL: Cardiff in South Wales.
INTERVIEWER: But you're very young. You must still be in your teens?
CAROL: Well, not quite. Actually I'm twenty-one. I've been dancing since I was five.
INTERVIEWER: Do you want to teach modern dance, Carol, or do you just want to perform?
CAROL: I just want to dance. That's all I care about at the moment. But one day, one day, I'd like to start my own dance group.
INTERVIEWER: Let's hope you achieve your ambition, Carol.
CAROL: Thanks.

Write

1. Ask the students questions to elicit the information which they will need to write their report. The students have studied how to report sentences using the present continuous, present simple, *going to* future and *can*, so ensure that the information you elicit does not use any other tenses. Point out to the students that *would like* does not change in reported speech.

Ask the students: *Where is Carol studying? Where is she from? What about her dancing career? What does she say she wants to do at the moment? And what is her ambition?*

MODEL ANSWER
Carol said (that) she was studying at the Madrid Centre for Modern Dance and (that) she was from Cardiff in South Wales. She said (that) she just wanted to dance at the moment but (that) she'd like to start her own dance group one day.

2. Ask the students to think about what they would most like to study after leaving school and where they would most like to study it. Tell them to imagine that they are doing that now. Give the class a few minutes to think about it and then ask them some questions – the type of questions asked in the interview in the tape, e.g: *What are you studying? Where are you studying? What is your ambition?* Put the students into pairs to ask each other questions. Tell them to adapt the comprehension questions from the listening exercise to help them.

Now ask the students to write a paragraph about themselves using the comprehension questions from the listening exercise as a guide.

Grammar summary

Remind students that:

- *to have* is contracted to *'ve* and *'s* in the table. It is usually contracted in the *have got to* structure.
- the form of the present perfect continuous is *have/has been + -ing*
- the present perfect continuous is used to refer to the duration of an activity that started in the past and continues up to the present and will probably continue into the future
- the verb in a direct sentence moves a step back into the past when it is reported using a reporting verb in the past.

Extra activities

1. Follow the trail

Put the students into teams and ask each team to draw a map of a small area somewhere near the school, either from memory or with the help of a local map. The team can choose the area to draw. They should then plan a route and write instructions to accompany the map, as they did for the Foxton trail. At the same time, they should plan a list of ten questions which could be answered by someone who followed the route on the map, e.g: *What's the name of the restaurant at the end of the High Street? What does the notice on the church door say?*

(The students may need to be given this as an extra task for homework so that some of them can walk the route and look out for things which would make good questions.) The teams then give each other the map, instructions and questions (if possible, make copies of these). Give the students one or two evenings, or a weekend, to answer each other's questions and then bring the teams back together to check through the answers and work out their scores. Award a point for each correct answer.

2. Treasure trail

Tell the students that the Foxton Trail is a treasure trail. Put them into teams and ask each team to decide where they have hidden the treasure. They must put it somewhere along the route, e.g: under a tree in the Brent Forest, inside one of the tents on the camping site. The teams then try to guess where each other's treasure is and take it in turns to ask each other Yes/No questions to find out if they are correct or if they are in the right area. The answer given can only be *Yes* or *No*, e.g: S1: *Is it somewhere in the village?* S2: *No.*

The team which is first to guess exactly where the other team's treasure is hidden is the winner.

Activity Book Key

Exercise 1

1. look after yourself
2. amuse yourself
3. build yourself
4. protect yourself
5. cheer yourself up
6. talked to myself

Exercise 2

1. I'm afraid I can't. I've got to go to judo class.
2. Sorry, I've got to go training.
3. No, I'm afraid I've got to visit Grandma.
4. I'm really sorry, Mark, I've got to babysit for Mum.
5. Yes, I've got to play volleyball.

Exercise 3

'I am annoyed because some students are always late. I think that it is time for a change and I hope that things are going to be different. I know that some students are always on time but there are others who are late two or three times a week. I am thinking of giving extra homework to people who are late more than once a week.'

Exercise 4

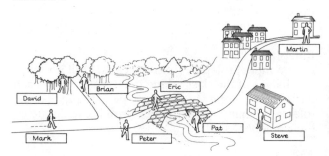

Exercise 5

1. She started two years ago.
2. It's about French rock bands.
3. She's got to/She has to write it in French.
4. She's got to/She has to write it in the Christmas holidays.
5. She wants information about young French rock bands and French rock music.

Exercise 6

Open exercise

📼 Speechwork Lessons 31–35

Pronunciation
Listen and repeat.
/f/ /f/ /f/   self, himself, herself

Listen and repeat.
/v/ /v/ /v/   selves, themselves, ourselves

Listen and repeat.
Did you enjoy yourself?
Yes, I did. So did Philip.
We both enjoyed ourselves.

Stress
Listen and repeat.
didida didida, didida didida, didida didida
I've been WORKing so HARD,
They've been EATing so MUCH,
She's been RUNning so WELL

Intonation
Listen and repeat.

How 'long have they been working here?

How 'long have you been waiting here?

How 'long has she been doing this?

Language use	Ask and talk about organisation
	Talk about products and materials
Grammar	Present simple passive:
	The cash box is kept in the safe.
	Costumes are worn on special nights.
	Butter is made from cream.
	My table is made of wood.
Vocabulary	bar plastic
	cash box safe
	cloakroom screen
	costume smuggler
	cotton wool
	eyepatch mark
	flour store
	leather type
	nylon gigantic
	omelette terrific
	pirate top

Background notes

Margate	A seaside town on the south-east coast of England.
Smugglers' and Pirates' Night	This means that anyone going to the disco on that night is expected to dress up as a smuggler or pirate. 'Smugglers' are a popular theme at seaside towns. The typical idea of a smuggler or pirate is someone dressed in baggy trousers, a striped T-shirt or brightly coloured shirt, a headscarf, large gold earrings and an eyepatch.
Rock videos	Videos to accompany pop records. They are also called 'pop videos'. See Lesson 39 for more information.
omelette	A hot dish made by beating up eggs and frying them in a frying pan. Cheese and other ingredients are often added.

Presentation

Write two sentences on the board, one in the active and one in the passive voice, e.g:
(1) They make Volvos in Sweden.
(2) Volvos are made in Sweden.
Clarify the concept of the passive construction. Point out to the students that in this case it is not important who makes the cars, so sentence (2) is better than sentence (1). We use the passive voice when the object, or recipient, of the action is more important than the subject, or doer.

Highlight the form of the passive construction. Point out that the object of the first, active sentence, *Volvos*, goes to the beginning of the second, passive sentence and becomes the subject. It is followed by the verb *to be* and the past participle of the main verb.

Drill the example sentence, *Volvos are made in Sweden,* and ask the students to tell you about other types of cars using the passive. Prompt them if necessary, e.g: T: *Renault.* S: *Renaults are made in France.* The students may go on to make sentences about other products or about food and drink and where they are made/produced/grown. As with the cars, give prompts for sentences if the students do not have many ideas of their own, e.g: T: *Sony video recorders.* S: *Sony video recorders are made in Japan.*

Write some of the example sentences on the board for the students to copy.

Picture

Ask questions about the picture and the advertisement to set the scene, e.g: *Why have the people in the background got scarves tied over their heads and large earrings in their ears? Why are they dressed up as pirates and smugglers? What is hanging from the ceiling?* etc. Explain *smugglers, pirates, gigantic, screen,* and give the students any other vocabulary that they want to know to answer the questions.

Dialogue and Exercise 1

Remind the students that Rick is working for the company *Anything Is Possible* and is sent to all sorts of different places to work. Ask them to listen to the tape to find out what Rick has to do in his latest job. With books closed, play the tape once and check the students' answers. Ask the students to read the questions in Exercise 1. Explain any unknown vocabulary needed to answer the questions, e.g: *cash box,* etc. The students then cover the dialogue in the book, listen again and discuss the answers to the questions in pairs. They then check their answers by referring to the dialogue in their books. Go through the answers with the class. Explain *eyepatch* and point out that eyepatches are associated with smugglers and pirates.

Ask the students to find the examples of the passive in the dialogue. The students then listen to the paused version of the dialogue and repeat.

Exercise 2

Practise the questions and answers T-S and then put the students into pairs. Check that they understand they should use the passive in their replies. When they have finished the questions, ask them if they can think of any more questions which they could ask about the school which would lead to an answer in the passive.

36

Exercise 3

Teach the vocabulary in the box using a picture, an object or the L1. Point out that we say an object is made *of* a certain material and that food or drink is made *from* certain ingredients.

Do the exercise T-S first. Students can reply with a short answer or a full sentence, e.g: T: *What's your desk made of?* S: *Wood./It's made of wood.* Put the students into pairs to ask each other. When they have finished, elicit full sentences from them for each question in the exercise, e.g: T: *Tell me about your shoes.* S: *My shoes are made of leather.* The students can then write the sentences in their notebooks.

Exercise 4

Put the students into small groups to discuss the questions in the book and to think of four more questions. The groups compare their answers to the questions in the book and then ask the other groups their own questions. This final stage could be played as a team game.

Exercise 5

Elicit a model roleplay from the whole class. Point out that when we are talking on the phone, we introduce ourselves by saying *It's (Alan) (here)* or *This is (Alan) (speaking)*. Put the students into pairs to practise their own roleplays.

Exercise 6

Tell the students to imagine that they went to Smugglers' Disco on Thursday night. Ask them questions about it, e.g: *Who did you go with? What did you wear?* etc. Put the students into pairs to ask each other. Then start the letter off on the board:

(Address)

(Date)

Dear Cathy,

How are you? Are you having a good time in London? Everything's OK here. A new disco opened in town just after you left. It's called Smugglers' Disco. I went there last Thursday.

The students complete the letter on their own.

 Oral exercises 1 and 2

Extra activities

1. Team game: passives only

Put the students into teams and ask each team to think of a process that they could describe, e.g. making a pot of tea/coffee, delivery of a letter. Go round and help the teams, providing any vocabulary that they need. A representative from each team then describes a process, using only sentences in the passive. Each team is given ten points to start off with and loses a point for each mistake in the passive construction or each time they forget to use a passive. At the end, you can award a maximum of five extra points for the accuracy of the description.

2. Class competition: design a disco

Ask the students to think of the type of disco they would like to see opening in their town. Tell them to think of a 'theme' for the disco in the way that 'smugglers' was the theme for the disco in this lesson. They should write and draw a description of how the disco will look and what the staff will wear. The students could do this individually or in groups.

Activity Book Key

Exercise 1

The video machines are kept in the games room and they are used a lot by our younger members. It costs 20p for a game, so sometimes the machines earn £20 or £30 a day. The machines are emptied every evening and the money is taken to the manager's office where it is counted. Then it is put in a cash box, which is kept in the manager's safe. On the following morning, it is sent to the bank.

Exercise 2

1. The parcels are kept in a large box.
2. They are counted at five o'clock each evening.
3. Stamps are put on them automatically.
4. The parcels are taken to the post office.
5. They are sent to several different countries.
6. They are sometimes sent in our own vans.

Exercise 3

1. money   2. animals   3. fish   4. clothes   5. books
6. money

Exercise 4

ring – This is made of gold.
shirt and stockings – These are made of nylon.
hat – This is made of wool.
car – This is made of metal, glass and plastic.
calendar – This is made of paper.
mirror – This is made of glass and wood.

Language use	Link past events
Grammar	Past perfect in contrast with past simple: *He realised he had forgotten* to buy a newspaper. *He had finished* his teaching for the summer term and *was* at the airport.
Vocabulary	anatomy pack check-in desk wonder kiosk lecture lecturer neighbour skeleton

Presentation

Tell the students a story about some robbers breaking into Smugglers' Disco. First, teach/revise the important vocabulary from the story, e.g: *robber, to break into, to steal, to climb.*

Tell the story: *Some robbers broke into Smugglers' Disco on Thursday night after the Smugglers' and Pirates' Night. They got into the disco by breaking the windows. They wanted to steal the money but they couldn't open the safe where the cash box was kept. They were very angry about this so they stole the video recorder and they drank all the whisky. Then they left. Someone saw them climbing out of the broken windows and telephoned the police. Five minutes later the police arrived.*

See if the class can retell the story with prompts from you where necessary. Then introduce the past perfect. Ask a question to provide a guide to meaning: *When the police arrived, were the robbers there? (No.) When the police arrived, the robbers had left.*

Point out that the action in the past perfect happened before the action in the past simple. Highlight the form: *had* + past participle. Ask the students what the police saw when they arrived. Elicit further examples of the past perfect, e.g: *The police saw that the robbers had broken the windows/stolen the video recorder/drunk all the whisky./Drill the examples of the past perfect, chorally and individually. Write on the board:

When the police arrived, the robbers had left.

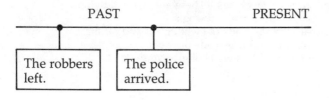

Point out that when there is a list of events in the past perfect in one sentence, and the subject is the same, there is no need to repeat *they had*, it is enough just to use the past participle, e.g. write on the board: *The police saw that the robbers had broken the windows, stolen the video recorder and drunk all the whisky.*

Ask students to study the example in the Look! box. Check their understanding.

Picture

Ask questions, e.g: *Where is the man? Why does he look surprised? Do you think it's his suitcase? Who do you think it belongs to?* Introduce/revise the important vocabulary, using the picture where possible, e.g: *suitcase, hand luggage, check-in desk, skeleton, lecturer.*

Text

Write a focus question on the board: *Why is there a skeleton in the suitcase?* The students read the text and answer the question. Students read the text again and find examples of the past perfect. Focus on each example and try to elicit in the L1 why the past perfect is used in each case.

Exercise 2

The students do the exercise orally in pairs. Check the answers with the whole class. Correct any tense errors.

Exercise 3

Elicit a model dialogue from the whole class first, then ask the students to write the dialogue. Students can act out the dialogue in pairs or groups of three. The third person can be a stranger who interrupts the conversation and tells the policeman that she/he has just found a skeleton in a suitcase.

MODEL DIALOGUE

LECTURER:	Officer, someone has taken my suitcase.
POLICEMAN:	I see. Where did you leave it?
LECTURER:	Near the check-in desk.
POLICEMAN:	Why?
LECTURER:	Because I realised I had forgotten to buy a newspaper and so I went over to the kiosk to get one.
POLICEMAN:	What does your case look like?
LECTURER:	It's a large brown suitcase.
POLICEMAN:	And what was in it?
LECTURER:	A skeleton.

Exercise 4

Ask the students if they have ever lost a suitcase or if they have ever put anything strange in a suitcase. Tell them that they are going to hear a story about a suitcase. Write a focus question on the board: *What did Susan put in her suitcase?*

37

Play the tape once and elicit the answer. Before the second playing, check students' understanding of the important words in the story, e.g. *to die, to bury, journey, tube, thief, gentleman*. Point out that when Susan says *What a gentleman*, she means that she thought he was very polite and well-mannered.

Ask students to read the questions in their books. Play the tape a second time for students to check their answers. Encourage the students to discuss how the man must have felt when he opened the suitcase and to say what they think about burying pets.

TAPESCRIPT

Listen to Susan telling a story. Look at your book and answer the questions.

SUSAN:

Well it's really rather a strange story and . . . and a bit sad. Recently my dog died – my dog Churchill. I was very fond of Churchill and I decided to bury him in my parents' garden because they've got a nice big garden and that way I'd be able to visit him as often as I wanted. The only problem was that my parents live a long way from me. They live on the other side of London. So to get to my parents' house I had to make a long journey by tube. So I put Churchill in my suitcase. I wrapped him up and I put him in my suitcase and I set off on my journey and I got to the underground and I bought my ticket and I started my journey. When I got to the other end, the escalator wasn't working so I had to walk up the stairs. But my suitcase was very heavy and I had a lot of other things – my handbag, my magazine – and the tube was very crowded, there were a lot of people, it was the rush-hour; and the whole thing was becoming very uncomfortable, when suddenly a man – a complete stranger – came up to me and asked if I needed any help. Well, that was wonderful! I thought: 'What a gentleman. How kind!' and I gave him my suitcase, and we started walking up the stairs. But he walked very very quickly – much more quickly than I could walk up the stairs – in fact he was going up two at a time, almost running, and I almost lost sight of him. In fact by the time I got to the top of the stairs, I'd lost him completely. He was nowhere to be seen. Now that's the rather sad bit because I thought the man was being very kind but in fact he was a thief. He'd stolen my suitcase. He wasn't being kind at all. Mind you I'd love to have seen the look on his face when he opened the suitcase and saw inside!

Exercise 5

Write a few questions on the board to guide the students' writing: *What happened to Susan's dog? What did she decide to do? How did she have to travel there? What did she do with the dog? What happened on the journey? Was the man a kind man or a thief? How do you think he felt when he opened the suitcase?*

MODEL ANSWER

Susan's dog died and she decided to bury him in her parents' garden. She had to go there by tube and so she put him in a suitcase. The suitcase was very heavy but a man offered to carry it. Susan gave him her suitcase but he walked very quickly and she lost him. He was a thief and he'd stolen her suitcase. When he got home and opened the suitcase, he was probably very surprised.

Oral exercises 3 and 4

Extra activities

1. Roleplay
Write the first two lines of a dialogue on the board:
CUSTOMS OFFICER: You said you had nothing to declare, didn't you?
TOURIST: Yes. I don't understand it. That wasn't in my suitcase this morning.
Explain *nothing to declare* and check that the students understand the tourist's reply. Then put them into pairs to continue the dialogue. When they have finished, ask a few of the pairs to act out their dialogues to the class.

2. When I got home the other night, . . .
Demonstrate this game with the whole class and then put the students into small groups to play it. The aim is for the students to say what they discovered when they got home, using the past perfect. First, they must repeat everything that has been said before. e.g:
S1: When I got home the other night, I couldn't believe my eyes. The dog had eaten the carpet.
S2: When I got home the other night, I couldn't believe my eyes. The dog had eaten the carpet and the cat had broken all the china.
etc.

Activity Book Key

Exercise 1
1. When I got to the office, it had closed.
2. Most people had gone home when we arrived at the party.
3. Someone had locked the cloakroom door and I couldn't get my coat.
4. We had bought some eggs so we made an omelette.
5. I ran to the cinema but they had gone in already.
6. I realised that someone had taken my bike.

Exercise 2
1. E   2. F   3. A   4. C   5. B   6. D

Exercise 3
1. B   2. D   3. J   4. C   5. E   6. G   7. A   8. F   9. H   10. I

Language use	Comprehension, summary and vocabulary skills	
Vocabulary	barrel	signal
	bay	stone
	candle	storeroom
	goods	explore
	graveyard	hold
	hole	asleep
	inn	secret
	passage	still
	shadow	except
	shore	

Background notes

Literary extract   The extract is taken from *Moonfleet*, by J. Meade Falkner, New Method Supplementary Readers Stage 3. It is a story about smuggling on the south coast of England in the eighteenth century.

🎧 Read and listen and Exercise 1

Explain to the students that they are going to hear an extract from a story about smuggling in the eighteenth century. Explain that *Moonfleet* is the name of a village (and of the book). Pre-teach a few essential items of vocabulary, e.g: *passage, smuggled goods, storeroom*. Write two focus questions on the board: *Who did the boat belong to? What did John Trenchard find at the end of the passage?* The students listen with their books closed and then answer the focus questions.

Read out the questions in Exercise 1 and explain any unknown vocabulary. See if the students can already answer any of the questions. The students then read the story and discuss the answers to the questions in pairs, using their dictionaries to check the meaning of any vocabulary which they need.

Exercise 2

Ask the students to look at the example sentence in the Look! box. Write a 'time line' on the board.

When I reached the graveyard, I began to feel afraid.

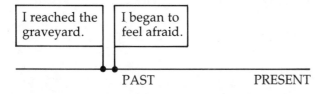

Explain that a *when* clause in the past simple with another clause in the past simple means either that

the two events happened at the same time, or they happened quickly one after the other. The event in the *when* clause happened first. The second event is often a result of the first one.

Point out that we put a comma after the *when* clause. Ask the students to write the complete sentences in their notebooks.

Exercise 3

Do the first two sentences and the last sentence orally with the whole class. Point out to students that John Trenchard's original thought: *Ah, I have found the smugglers' storeroom* becomes: *He knew (that) he had found the smugglers' storeroom*. When the reporting verb (e.g. *know, say, think, hope*) is in the past, the original thought or speech goes a step further back into the past: the present perfect and past simple go into the past perfect.

Explain to the students that in order to do the exercise, they sometimes need to add a connecting word not provided in the outline. Ask them to use *because* in Sentence 4 and to use *and* in Sentences 5 and 6.

Ask the students to write the complete summary in their notebooks. Listen to a few students reading their summaries and correct any mistakes. Example: *1. One night John Trenchard decided to explore a/the secret passage in the graveyard of Moonfleet. 2. When he reached the graveyard, he felt afraid.*

Extra activities

1. Roleplay: John Trenchard meets the smugglers!
Tell the students to imagine that the smugglers find John Trenchard in their secret storeroom. Elicit a few ideas on what the smugglers might do. Put the students into groups of three to five and appoint one of the group to be John Trenchard and the others to be the smugglers. Students roleplay the scene.

You may wish to give each of the smugglers a card with their opinion on it to ensure that the smugglers have some argument about what to do, e.g:
1. You think that John Trenchard should be killed. It is the only safe thing to do.
2. You are John Trenchard's uncle. (He didn't know until now that you were a smuggler). You want to make sure that he is not hurt. You would like him to agree to accept some money and not say anything about what he has found.
3. John Trenchard is the first person to find your secret storeroom so you think he's obviously very clever. You think he might be a useful member of your group and you would like him to join you.

38

4. You don't want to kill John Trenchard but you think it would be a good idea to frighten him and make sure that he doesn't tell anyone what he has found. You would like to shut him in the storeroom for one or two days and then say that he can go if he doesn't tell anyone about the storeroom.

2. Finishing the sentence

Write on the board ten *when* clauses. Do not write the second clause, only the *when* clause, e.g: *When they saw the police* . . .

Divide the class into teams. Ask the teams to finish each of the sentences on the board, using the past simple, e.g: When they saw the police, they ran away. The teams then read out the complete sentences. Award a point for each correct, logical sentence.

Activity Book Key

 Exercise 1

TAPESCRIPT

Look at your book. Listen to the conversation in a smugglers' cave and write the answers to the questions.

NED: All right, not far to go now. Drat! I think we're here. Yes, this is it. Now come on in, and hurry up!

JACK: Stop it, Pete, that's my foot!

PETE: Sorry . . .

NED: Shut up, will you. Now, are we all here, Jack?

JACK: Yes.

NED: Pete?

PETE: Yup.

NED: Madge?

MADGE: I'm here too.

NED: Good, that's it then. Now, do you all know what to do?

PETE: I'm frightened, Ned.

NED: We're all frightened. Just do what I say and it'll be all right. No one knows we're here. And no one knows what we're going to do. So just keep calm and don't panic and we'll be all right.

ALL: Right.

NED: I'll just go over the plans. The boat's kept on the beach, and the gold is under the tree on the island. We take the boat and get the guns from Jack's house. Then we get the barrels from Pete's house, and we go over to the island to pick up the gold. Is that understood?

ALL: Yes, that's fine.

NED: Now, after that . . . Did you hear something?

MADGE: It's the church bell!

NED: We've got to get out of this cave! Let's go.

JOHN: Have they gone?

PAULA: Yes, they've gone. What's going on?

JOHN: I don't know, but I think we'd better tell the customs men.

KEY

1. four 2. afraid 3. No.
4. the boat – on the beach
   the gold – under the tree on the island
   the guns – in Jack's house
5. They hear the church bell.

Exercise 2

1. packet 2. barrel 3. box 4. can/tin 5. bottle
6. suitcase 7. handbag 8. wallet

Exercise 3

ACROSS 3. fail 4. send 5. perform 8. look
9. pass
DOWN 1. give 2. wear 5. pack 6. ring 7. miss

Exercise 4

Open exercise

MODEL QUESTIONS
1. What are pop videos called in the United States?
2. Where is the best place to go if you want to make a pop video?
3. Why are they a very important part of the record business?/Why are they like advertisements?
4. What are the two kinds of pop video?/What kinds of pop video are there?
5. What is a 'performance' video?
6. How long do pop videos last?
7. Are they cheap to make?

Language use	Specify things
Grammar	Defining relative clauses with *where*: This is a video *where the performers play and sing their song.*
Vocabulary	amplifier disappear backing group include business promote cave set charts conceptual dock empty failure exotic loudspeaker several microphone tropical orchestra therefore pony where pop video at the moment setting the bit . . . warehouse

Background notes

promos   An abbreviation for 'promotional videos'.

clip   Besides being the American for 'pop video', 'clip' is also used to refer to an excerpt from a film, a 'film clip'.

conceptual video   A video which aims to give its viewers the idea or concept of the music being played or listened to. It tries to create a distinctive atmosphere and is sometimes like a fantasy world.

Read and answer

Use the picture to introduce the theme. Ask questions, e.g: *What are the people doing in this picture? What does the room look like? Do you like it? Why do bands make pop videos? What do you think of pop videos? Do you like them?*

As you discuss the picture with the students, introduce some of the new vocabulary, e.g: *pop video, cave, setting, advertisement, to promote (records).* Students read the focus questions and the text and then answer the focus questions.

Exercise 1

Students read the passage again and note down any vocabulary they would like to know the meaning of. Ask them to try to deduce meaning from context and then to check it in their dictionaries. Provide explanations where necessary. The students then do the exercise. Ask them to refer back to the text as necessary.

Presentation

Ask the students what a 'performance video' is to elicit the sentence from the reading passage: *This is a video where the performers play and sing their song.* If the students cannot produce this sentence, ask them to refer back to the reading passage to answer your question. Write the sentence on the board. Explain the use of the relative clause. Elicit or point out that:

● the relative clause is . . . *where the performers play and sing their song*

● it is a defining relative clause. The main clause does not have any real meaning without it. The relative clause describes the video and tells us which video is being talked about

● *where* refers back to the video. It means that the performers play and sing *in the video.*

Prompt the students into giving you another example of the structure to check their understanding, e.g. say: *A lot of pop videos are made in London. Give me a sentence starting with 'London is a city . . .'* Elicit: *London is a city where a lot of pop videos are made.*

Note: Relative clauses with *where* should not be completely new to the students. An example was introduced to them in Lesson 1. The second relative clause with *where* in the reading passage is a non-defining relative clause: *The other is called a 'conceptual' video, where the music is played in a strange or exotic setting . . . .* The sentence makes sense without the relative clause. Non-defining relative clauses are preceded by a comma. *Where* can usually be replaced by *in which.*

Exercise 2

Draw students' attention to the Look! box. Ask them to write the complete sentences in their notebooks.

39

Exercise 4
Ask the class about their favourite and least favourite videos and encourage them to use: *I (especially) like/don't like the bit where . . .* Ask them who the performers are, where the video is set and what sort of things the performers do. (This will help to prepare them for Exercise 5.) Then put them into groups for the discussion. Check that they understand *latest*. Ask one person from each group to report back to the class at the end.

Exercise 5
Elicit a complete model paragraph about one of the students' favourite videos, using the guidelines in the Students' Book. Write it on the board. The students then write their own paragraph about a different video.

(If you can show an example of a pop video, this would be very helpful. If you think the students will not be able to write about a pop video, ask them to write about a film instead.)

Extra activities

1. Team Quiz
Put the students into teams and ask them to think of definitions of places using relative clauses with *where*. The teams then take turns to give a definition and the other teams say what the place is. A point is given for each correct definition and each correct answer, e.g: *It's a place where children and teenagers study.* (A school.) *It's a place where you stay if you're ill.* (A hospital.)

2. Listen to records
Ask the students to bring in a favourite cassette of rock music with English words. Choose a song and transcribe the words before the lesson as the words of songs are often difficult to hear. In the following lesson, play some of the songs to the class. Then play your chosen song again and see if the students can pick out the words. Check that the students have written down the words correctly. They may then like to sing along with the song, but do not force them to do so if they do not want to. The students can discuss the content of a suitable pop video to accompany the song.

Activity Book Key

Exercise 1
Open exercise

Vocabulary	amazement	fix
	audience	pay
	mattress	place
	screen	project
	studio	report
	taxi fare	support
	waistcoat	yawn
	wall	horizontal
	attach	in case
	film	
Speechwork	Pronunciation: /r/ mirror	
	Stress: dadidi dadidi, SOMEone had TAKen it	
	Intonation: I 'realised that 'someone had taken it.	

Background notes

'Top of the Pops' A weekly TV pop music programme featuring bands or singers with records in the top 100. The studio audience are filmed dancing to the records.

Roleplay

Explain any unknown vocabulary. Elicit a model dialogue from the class and drill it with two halves of the class taking a part each. Then put the students into pairs to roleplay the conversation. Write a model dialogue on the board at the end, eliciting it from the students, and ask them to copy it into their notebooks.

Note: The present simple as future is used in the dialogue:

YOU: Oh, fine. And *do we get paid?*
SHANE: No, but *we are given* a hot meal and our taxi fare home.

The present simple can be used to refer to the future when we are talking about official arrangements or arrangements made by an organisation or company.

Word study

Students use their dictionaries to check the meanings of any unknown verbs in the box. They write the complete sentences in their notebooks.

KEY
1. . . . so she *hid* it.
2. . . . he *placed* them . . .
3. . . . we all *dressed in* some funny clothes.
4. . . . they *covered* the floor *with* old newspapers.
5. He *fixed* the notice firmly to a tree with a nail.
6. . . . they *built* a fence . . .
7. . . . he *supported* it . . .

Listen

With books shut, ask students if they have seen 'Superman' or 'Supergirl' and how they think they 'fly' in the films. Listen to their ideas and then ask them to open their books and look at the diagrams. Students then try to describe to you how the effect is achieved, without looking at the text. Remind them of the vocabulary they used in the word study and prompt them into using it. Explain *to attach* and *to project*.

Play the tape and ask the students to look at the diagrams as they listen. The students then read the text, look up any unknown vocabulary in their dictionaries and copy and complete the paragraph. They compare their answers in pairs. Play the tape again for students to check their answers. Point out that the listening text on tape is not exactly the same as the text in the Students' Book, but it does provide all the information that the students need to fill in the gaps.

TAPESCRIPT

Listen to a special effects technician from a film studio describing how the actors who play people like Superman, Supergirl and Santa Claus are made to fly. Look at your book and copy and complete the paragraph using the correct form of the verbs.

TECHNICIAN:

Say I want someone to fly over the Niagara Falls. First the Niagara Falls are filmed from a helicopter. Then we build a wall and we cover it with a great big screen. The actor or actress is dressed in a steel waistcoat, which is hidden by his or her costume. Attached to the steel waistcoat is a horizontal steel bar which supports the actor but which can't be seen from the front. The bar is then fixed securely to the wall, high up on the screen. This is going to be the flying position. The actor is then put in position approximately fifty metres off the ground. Of course, lots of soft mattresses are placed underneath in case the actor falls. The background film of the Niagara Falls is projected on to the screen and then the actor's body movements and the background film are combined and filmed together so that background and foreground are seen as one. Now the actor appears to be flying.

Write

Explain/revise *to yawn, amazement, lion* and *to face*. Ask the students to read the story outline. Elicit an example story from the class. Check that the students know what tense should be used in each sentence. Check that they remember the difference between the past simple, past continuous and past perfect. The students then write their own stories in their notebooks and read them out to each other in groups.

Dictionary skills

Numbers 1, 2, 4 and 6 are wrong. The correct spellings are: 1. skeleton 2. textbook
4. forgotten 6. business

40

Grammar summary

Remind students that:

- the passive is formed with the verb *to be* and the past participle. It is used when the doer of the action is unknown or is less important than the action and/or the recipient of the action
- the past perfect is used to describe an event which happened before another event in the past simple
- in reported speech, if the reporting verb is in the past, the verb in the reported sentence is one step further back in the past than the original thought or speech. Therefore, the present simple becomes the past simple, the present continuous becomes the past continuous, and the present perfect and past simple become the past perfect
- the relative pronoun *where* means *in which*.

Extra activities

1. Superman/Supergirl for a day

Students imagine that they can be Superman or Supergirl for a day. They can perform one act and they should decide on their own or in pairs what act they think would be the most useful to their town, country or the world. Each student or pair of students then reports their ideas to the class. Encourage some class discussion.

2. Looking at special effects

Students think of an interesting special effect they have seen at the cinema or on television. Ask them to describe and/or draw it in their project books and write how they think it was achieved. Or they could discuss 'stunts' which they have seen on television or at the cinema and describe to each other what they were and how they think they were done, e.g. someone jumping from a building on fire, a car going over a cliff.

Activity Book Key

Exercise 1
1. She was tired because she had been to a rock concert on Sunday.
2. He was worried because he hadn't done his homework on Sunday.
3. She was happy because she had met Rick in Dover on Sunday.
4. He was pleased because the school football team had won a silver medal on Sunday.
5. She went to the doctor because she had hurt her arm on Sunday.
6. He felt ill because he had eaten six hamburgers on Sunday.

Exercise 2
1. Yes, it's kept in the sitting room.
2. Yes, it's used every day.
3. Yes, the tapes are stored in this cupboard.
4. Yes, it's cleaned every week.

5. Yes, it's switched off at night.
6. Yes, I think it's used too much.

Exercise 3
NYLON	LEATHER
GLASS	PLASTIC
COTTON	WOOD
WOOL	PAPER

Exercise 4
1. vacuum cleaner 2. car 3. fridge 4. stereo system/hi-fi system/music centre 5. typewriter 6. iron

Exercise 5
1. These are kept in the kitchen and are used to cut food.
2. This is kept in the kitchen and is used to cook food.
3. This is kept in the bathroom and is used to wash your hair.
4. This is kept in a bank and is used to keep money in.
5. This is kept in a wallet or a purse and is used to buy things.
6. This is kept in a classroom and is used to clean the blackboard.

Exercise 6
1. You can take up to 20 kg.
2. Yes, you can, up to 5 kg.
3. You put it under the seat or in the locker above the seat.
4. Yes, you can.
5. No, please remove all old labels.
6. Yes, you do.
7. Please pack it in your carry-on baggage.

Speechwork Lessons 36–40

Pronunciation
Listen and repeat.
/r/ /r/ /r/ mirror tomorrow nearer

Listen and repeat.
Where's the mirror?
I'll bring it tomorrow.
(Note: Point out that the final *r* in *mirror* and *nearer* is not pronounced in British English. The final sound in these two words is a schwa /ə/.)

Stress
Listen and repeat.
dadidi dadidi, dadidi dadidi, dadidi dadidi
SOMEone had TAKen it,
PETer had BORrowed it,
SUSan had STOLen it

Listen and repeat.
I wanted the narrow mirror,
But someone had taken it.

Intonation
Listen and repeat.

I 'realised that 'someone had taken it.

I 'thought that 'someone had stolen it.

I 'hoped that 'someone had borrowed it.

You'd better watch it!

Language use	Give advice and warning Apologise and explain Accept apologies
Grammar	Modal *had better*: *You'd better go* without him. *You'd better not be* late again. The present perfect with *first/ second time*: *This isn't the first time he's been late.*
Vocabulary	puncture by accident get into trouble instead get the sack urgently had better Hi folks! knock over Watch it! oversleep sour suspicious

Presentation

Draw a picture of an untidy person. Tell the students that this person is going for a job interview at a bank next week. Ask them if they think he will get the job. Elicit details about his appearance, e.g. his hair is long, his shoes are dirty, his clothes have got holes in them, he has got a long beard. Tell the students that they are a friend of this person and they are giving advice. Provide a model sentence, e.g: *You'd better have a haircut.* Clarify meaning and form and check students' understanding.

Point out, in the L1 if necessary, that:

- *you'd better* is used to give strong advice or a warning
- it is generally used with people we know well
- *you'd* is short for *you had*
- *you'd better* is followed by the infinitive without *to*
- the negative is *you'd better not* + infinitive.

Drill the model sentence. Elicit other example sentences, using the same situation. Provide prompts if necessary, e.g: T: *His clothes are very old.* S: *You'd better not wear those clothes*, etc. Drill the example sentences and then write them on the board.

🔊 Dialogue

Students look at the picture and guess what is happening. Ask questions to guide them: *What is this place? Who's just arriving? How does the other man look? Who do you think he is? Why do you think he is angry?*

The students then listen to the dialogue with their books closed and check that their guesses are correct.

Explain *puncture, sour, to get the sack* and any other unknown vocabulary. Play the first half of the dialogue again. Ask the students what Tony says to

Andrea about Rick's lateness. Elicit: *This isn't the first time he's been late.* Point out that the present perfect is used after *This is(n't) the first/second time . . . .* Drill the example sentence. Ask students to copy it into their notebooks from the Look! box.

The students then listen to the paused version of the dialogue and repeat.

Exercise 1

Ask the students to complete the conversation in writing and then to practise reading it aloud in pairs. Explain: *to get into trouble, to oversleep* and *I know what it's like*.

Exercise 2

Do the exercise orally with the whole class first and practise the dialogues T–S and S–S in front of the class. Refer students to the example sentences in the Look! box to help them. Then put the students into pairs to practise.

Exercise 3

When the students have written the apologies with their responses, they practise reading them out in pairs. A number of variations are possible.

Exercise 4

MODEL ANSWER
You'd better go and apologise to her.
You'd better get some new bike lights.
You'd better not go out on your bike in the dark again.
You'd better offer to pay for a new light for her car.
You'd better be more careful in future.

Exercise 5

Say to the students: *Jane is in London. It's her first visit there. What can she say starting with 'This is . . .'?*. Elicit *This is the first time I've been to (or I've visited) London.* Students read the exercise. Check that they understand the vocabulary. Revise the past participle form of all the verbs. Refer them to the example sentence in the Look! box to remind them of the structure. Do the exercise orally with the whole class, drilling each sentence chorally and individually. Then ask the students to write the sentences in their notebooks.

Exercises 6 and 7

Elicit an example of the roleplay from the whole class and then put the students into pairs to practise it. When they have finished, students write the conversation in their notebooks.

MODEL ROLEPLAY
A: Good morning. I'm sorry I'm late. I overslept.
B: That's all right, but you'd better not oversleep tomorrow because your group is leaving early to go to Brighton.
A: Oh yes. Don't worry. I won't oversleep tomorrow.

 Oral exercises 1 and 2

Extra activities

1. Split dialogues
Divide the class into groups of five or six. Give each student one half of a two-line dialogue with either a problem or a *You'd/We'd better* . . . response. Ask the group to say their sentences to each other until they find their partner. When they have found her or him, they should decide who the two speakers are, what their relationship is to each other (e.g. parent and child, police officer and suspect, two friends) and what the situation is. They should then make up a further two lines of the conversation.
You can provide dialogues like these:
1. A: Look, it's after midnight and Alison's still not home.
   B: I think we'd better phone the police.
2. A: I can't stand up any longer. I think I'm going to faint.
   B: You'd better sit down.

2. Guess the first sentence
Give the students a response using *had/'d better* and ask them to guess what was said to get this response. You could put the students into teams for this activity and award a point to the first team which makes a suitable suggestion.
Examples:
1. You'd better take an aspirin. (I've got a headache.)
2. Well, you'd better go to bed early. (I've got to get up really early tomorrow.)

Activity Book Key

Exercise 1
Open exercise

Exercise 2
1. aeroplane 2. field 3. eyes 4. burn 5. right
6. flour 7. kitten 8. leather

Language use	Make logical deductions
Grammar	Modal verbs: *can't might, could* and *must + be* *It can't be* from Gran. *It might be* from Cindy. *It could be* chocolates. *It must be* the postman. Adverb *probably*: It's *probably* chocolates.
Vocabulary	bulb plant detective probably postmark on the other shape hand tulip bulb weather forecast whistle

Materials

A wrapped object for the students to feel.

Presentation

Find an article which has an interesting shape and texture, and perhaps an interesting sound, e.g: a child's toy, a clock, kitchen utensil, a tube of toothpaste, some uncooked spaghetti, a handbag mirror, a bath plug. Wrap it up in several layers of paper. Hold the package up for the students to see and shake it. Ask them to guess what it is to elicit: *It might/could be . . .*, e.g: *It could/might be a book*. Then give it to the students to feel and shake and gradually to unwrap. Use their guesses to provide further examples of *It could/might be . . .* and to introduce examples of *It can't be . . .* and *It must be . . .*, e.g: *It can't be a book (because it's got something in it), It must be a clock (because I can hear it ticking)*. Drill each example sentence.

Point out that this structure is used to make logical deductions. We make guesses based on the information we have. We use *must be* (positive) and *can't be* (negative) when we feel sure and *might/could be* when we think something is possible. Write example sentences on the board.

Text

Pre-teach *whistle, postmark, shape, tulip bulbs, to plant, probably*. Write a focus question on the board: *What's in the parcel?* The students read the text and answer the question. See if students can guess the meaning of *On the other hand . . . .* If not, explain.

Exercise 1

Students quickly read the text again. They then cover up the text and the Look! box. Explain *detective* and ask them to discuss the answers to the

questions in pairs. Check through the answers with the class and, as you do so, elicit the examples of the language of deduction used in the text, e.g:

T: Question 3: Why did Kate think it might be from their grandmother?
S: Because she often sends them parcels.
T: Yes. And what did Kate say?
S: 'It might be from Gran.'

Drill the example sentences. Then ask students to uncover the Look! box and study the examples. Students can copy them into their notebooks.

Exercise 2

Ask the students to make their guesses in pairs and then report back to the class. If possible, the students should give reasons for their guesses to reinforce their understanding of the use of the structures *might/could/can't/must be . . .*, e.g: *It might be a telephone receiver because it's round and it's got holes in it.*

ANSWERS A toothbrush and a telephone receiver.

Exercise 3

Elicit suggestions about the first picture from the whole class and make corrections as necessary. Prompt the students into using the *might/could/can't/must be . . .* structure, e.g: S1: *He must be over sixty*. S2: *No, he can't be*. Put the students into pairs to discuss the woman in the second picture. After the discussion, tell the students that the man is a fisherman from southern Italy and the woman lives on a farm on a Scottish island.

Exercise 4

Ask the class for their guesses and, if necessary, prompt them into using *It might/could be . . .*

ANSWER An Australian aboriginal dance.

🖭 Exercise 5

Play the first scene and ask the class where they think it might be. Prompt them into using *It might/could/can't/must be . . .* and ask them to give reasons. Then play the following scenes. Pause the tape after every few lines and ask students to make guesses. Explain new vocabulary if necessary.

Note: When the man asks the girl if she wants One, Two or Three in scene number five, he is asking her which screen number she wants. Many cinemas in Britain are divided into three and show three different films.

He asks her whether she is over fifteen because the film she has chosen cannot be seen by children under fifteen. There is a censors' rating system in Britain and there are four classifications: 18 – over 18, 15 – over 15, PG – parental guidance recommended, U – unclassified.

42

TAPESCRIPT
Listen to these scenes. Say where you think they might be and why.

1.
CASHIER: How would you like it?
CUSTOMER: Five tens and two fives please.
CASHIER: Five tens and two fives. There you are.
CUSTOMER: Thank you. Oh, look. Can you change the five pound note into coins, please?
CASHIER: Of course. And some silver?
CUSTOMER: Please. Thank you very much.

2.
CUSTOMER: Um, how much are those nice big yellow ones?
ASSISTANT: One pound fifty each.
CUSTOMER: OK. I'll have three.
ASSISTANT: Anything else?
CUSTOMER: Yes, I think I'd like some green to go with it.
ASSISTANT: What about some of this fern?
CUSTOMER: Mm, fine.
ASSISTANT: Do you want to write a card to go with it?
CUSTOMER: Yes, it's for a birthday.
ASSISTANT: Here you are.
CUSTOMER: Oh, thanks.
ASSISTANT: That'll be five pounds altogether.

3.
CUSTOMER: I'd like something for my cold, please. A bottle of Sleepwell and some aspirin. And can you recommend something for a sore throat?
CHEMIST: Why don't you try these new throat pastilles. They're menthol, lemon and honey.
CUSTOMER: Mmm. They sound nice. I'll try a packet. Oh, and some paper tissues too, please.

4.
POLICEWOMAN: Right. I'll just get a report form for your statement. Can I have your name and address please?
MR MAYNARD: John Maynard, with a Y, 43 Delemere Road.
POLICEWOMAN: That's just round the corner, isn't it? And is that where the car was parked?
MR MAYNARD: Yes. Right outside the house.
POLICEWOMAN: And are you the owner of the car, sir?
MR MAYNARD: Yes, but my wife drives it during the day.
POLICEWOMAN: Now, when did she last see the car?

5.
GIRL 1: Two please.
MAN: Which one do you want? One, Two or Three?
GIRL 2: We want Number Two please: 'The Bride of Dracula'.
MAN: Are you over fifteen?
GIRL 1: Course we are.
MAN: You don't look it. Have you got any identification?
GIRL 2: No. What about the one showing in Number Three?

MAN: 'Young Sherlock Holmes'? Yes, you can get into that.
GIRL 2: OK, then.

KEY
1. a bank   2. a flower shop   3. a chemist's
4. a police station   5. a cinema (foyer)

 Oral exercise 3

Extra activities

1. What is it?
Give the students definitions of well-known objects, building the definition sentence by sentence. Ask the students to make guesses after each sentence, either individually or in teams. Award a point for each correct use of the language of deduction and three points for the correct answer. After you have given the students one or two definitions, they can write their own and continue playing the game against each other, e.g:
It has a round shape. (It might be a ball or it might be an orange.)
It's flat. (It can't be a ball or an orange. It might be a plate.)
It's black. (It can't be a plate. It might be a button.)
It has circular lines/grooves on it. (It might be a tyre. It can't be a button.)
It plays music. (It must be a record.)

2. Discussing photographs
Ask the students to bring in photographs of friends or relatives to show to each other so that they can guess who the people are as they did in Exercise 3. This could be done as a game in groups with students awarding points to each other for correct guesses.

Activity Book Key

Exercise 1
It's a dinosaur.

Exercise 2
So who is stealing the money? It can't be Mrs Robbins because she doesn't have the key to the cash box. It might/could be Mr Rix, as he has a key, but he must know that we are watching him all the time. It can't be his assistant because she doesn't have a key either, although she might/could borrow it from him sometimes. No, it can't be her because she's on holiday at the moment. There's only one person who has the opportunity and that's Mr Rix. It must be him.

Exercise 3
COLD: milkshake, ice-lolly, bitter, fridge, cool, freezing, Arctic, snow, ice
HEAT: boiling, barbecue, cooking, microwave, hot, tropical, burning, fire, baking, match

Language use	Comprehension, summary and vocabulary skills	
Vocabulary	adaptor	investigate
	appointment	mend
	bow tie	stare
	detective	trace
	dollar bill	attractive
	electric razor	elementary
	eyesight	old-fashioned
	felt tip pen	rude
	optician	rather
	spectacle case	usually

Background notes

Literary extract The extract is taken from *The Return of Sherlock Holmes* by Sir Arthur Conan Doyle, New Method Supplementary Readers Stage 3. The book includes three cases for Sherlock Holmes to solve: *The Six Napoleons*, *The Norwood builder* and *The golden glasses*. The extract is taken from *The golden glasses*.

Sherlock Holmes See Background notes, Lesson 33.

five-star hotel Hotels in Britain are awarded stars. Five stars are the maximum so a five-star hotel is a hotel of a very high standard.

an electric razor with an adaptor The adaptor allows the razor to be used in another country, which has different sockets for the electricity supply.

Read and listen and Exercise 1

Ask the students to tell you what they know about Sherlock Holmes. Students read the introduction to the text and look at the picture. Ask them for ideas on what Sherlock Holmes may be able to find out from the pair of glasses. The students then read and listen to the text to find out.

Write on the board the vocabulary to be introduced/revised from the text, e.g: *close together, stares*, etc. Students read the text again to try to deduce the meaning of the vocabulary from context. Check their understanding of the vocabulary and explain it where necessary. Tell the students that *Elementary, my dear Watson* is Sherlock Holmes's most famous line. Watson is always amazed by Holmes's brilliance and this is the reply that Holmes often gives.

Explain any unknown vocabulary in Exercise 1. The students do the exercise.

Ask the students to pick out the two examples of the *must be* . . . structure from the text.

Exercise 3

Ask the students to read the exercise and explain any unknown vocabulary to them, e.g: *five-star hotel, to trace*, etc. In groups, students discuss the information. The activity should be fairly free and the students may reach a number of different conclusions. Ask each group to report back at the end and to give reasons for their conclusions. Encourage them to use the language of deduction: *might/could/can't/must be . . .* Each student should then write a note to the policeman.

MODEL ANSWER
Try to find a man who is quite smartly dressed and probably middle-aged because his suitcase is old-fashioned. He might have a small beard or moustache because he left his razor in the hotel. He must be a foreigner because his razor had an adaptor. He could be American because he left a few dollar bills. He must wear glasses because he left a spectacle case in the room. And he must like living a good life because the hotel was five-star and we found a bow tie, an opera programme and an empty bottle of champagne. He must be left-handed because he wrote a telephone number on the left-hand side of the mirror. And he must be tall because he wrote it at the top. It might be the number of a friend so you should phone the number.

Extra activities

1. Guess who it is

Put the students into teams. Ask each team to think of the name of a famous person and to note down some information about that person. The teams then give one piece of information at a time. The other team(s) must make a deduction from that information using *might/could/can't/must be . . .* Point out to the students that in this context it is more natural to say *It might/could be* + noun/pronoun than *He . . .* or *She . . .* Award a point for each correct sentence which uses the structure and five extra points if the students find the right answer before the fifth piece of information, e.g:

TEAM A: He comes from the United States.
TEAM B: He must be American.
TEAM A: He's an actor.
TEAM B: It might be Sylvester Stallone.
TEAM A: He's also a politician.
TEAM B: It could be Ronald Reagan, etc.

2. Write about a detective story

Talk to the students about detective stories they have read or seen on television or at the cinema. Ask the students to write a summary of one of their favourites in their project book.

43

Activity Book Key

🔲 **Exercise 1**

Look at your book. Listen to the conversations. Write where you think each conversation is happening.

1.

SINGER:	And all I want to do is love you. How was that? Was that OK?
PRODUCER:	Yes, that's very good, darling, but, er, can we have a bit more oomph in it. And all I want to do is love you.
SINGER:	And all I want to do is love you.
PRODUCER:	Yes, that's a bit too much. Don't go over the top. And again.
SINGER:	And all I want to do is love you.
PRODUCER:	That's great! Fantastic! Hold it like that, and we'll do it again with the rest of the band music.
SINGER:	Yeah . . . OK. And all I want to do is love you.
PRODUCER:	Perfect! Five minutes coffee break, everybody!

2.

SURGEON:	Scalpel . . . scissors . . . right, we cut the skin here . . . tie it back . . . forceps. It's important to cut cleanly and quickly. Make the hole as large as you want. How's the patient, Doctor?
ANAESTHETIST:	Oxygen/air balance is fine.
SURGEON:	Good. Can I have a bit more light here, please? Mmm . . . Have you watched any heart operations before, Dr Clark?
DR CLARK:	No, this is my first.
SURGEON:	Well, I'll keep talking then. You cut the artery here and tie it back like this . . .

3.

SOUND TRACK	
CROWD NOISE:	Let's go to the castle.
MONSTER:	What do you want of me?
STUDIO	
EDITOR 1:	Hold it. Can you stop the film there. Isn't there a roll of thunder here?
EDITOR 2:	Here? I don't think so. Hang on a minute. Oh, yes, there is. Just before he says 'What do you want?' I'll wind it back. *(Soundtrack repeated.)*
EDITOR 1:	Here. Just before he speaks.
EDITOR 2:	Mmm . . . What sort of thunder? Quiet or loud?
EDITOR 1:	Sort of medium thunder, I think.
EDITOR 2:	Right. Here it is. *(Soundtrack repeated with thunder.)*
EDITOR 1:	Great.

4.

ATTENDANT:	Oi!
BOY:	Pardon?
ATTENDANT:	I said 'Oi!' Have you got a ticket?
BOY:	Yes, sure. Here it is.
ATTENDANT:	Right. Put your clothes in one of those lockers, and tie the key to your swimming costume. And you have to have a shower before you go into the pool.
BOY:	OK.
ATTENDANT:	Kids!

KEY

1. It might be a recording studio.
2. It might be (a room in) a hospital/an operating theatre.
3. It might be a film/television studio.
4. It might be a swimming pool.

Exercise 2

1. usual, unusual, usually, unusually
2. successful, unsuccessful, successfully, unsuccessfully
3. fortunate, unfortunate, fortunately, unfortunately
4. pleasant, unpleasant, pleasantly, unpleasantly
5. regular, irregular, regularly, irregularly
6. healthy, unhealthy, healthily, unhealthily

Exercise 3

PART A Open exercise
PART B 1. washing powder 2. coffee bags
3. a flash for a camera 4. milk powder

The patterns in Peru

Language use	Ask and talk about historical facts
Grammar	Past simple passive: *When were the Nazca lines discovered? They were discovered in 1939.*
Vocabulary	area invent base launch battle remain desert accurate pilot alien position astonishing runway geometric spacecraft huge theory mysterious tomb prehistoric

Background notes

BC Before Christ. This is written after the number of the year, e.g. *300 BC*.

AD Anno Domini, the year of our Lord. This is used for the years since Christ's birth. It is written before or after the number of the year, e.g. *AD 900* or *900 AD*.

Presentation

Revise the present passive, which was introduced in Lesson 36. Practise the structure orally, asking the students to convert sentences from the active into the passive, e.g: *They make Fiat cars in Italy. (Fiat cars are made in Italy.) They make butter from milk. (Butter is made from milk.)* Write one example on the board and point out how the passive is formed. Then introduce the past passive. Write a sentence on the board in the past simple active, e.g: *They took the injured woman to hospital.* Ask the students to change the sentence into the passive. Elicit: *The injured woman was taken to hospital.* Help the students if necessary. Point out that:

- the past passive is formed with *was/were* + past participle
- a question is formed with *was/were* + receiver of action + past participle, e.g: *When was the house built?*
- the passive is used when the action or recipient of the action is more important than the person or thing which performed it, or when we do not know who or what performed it
- we can say who or what performed the action if we add *by* + the name of the person/thing, e.g: *The new hospital was opened by the Queen.*

Do another exercise orally to check that the students have understood and to give them more practice. Ask the students to convert sentences from the active to the passive, e.g: *Someone stole my car last week. (My car was stolen last week.)*

They built the school in 1950. (The school was built in 1950.)
I didn't use my bike last year. (My bike wasn't used last year.)
Did someone buy this bread yesterday? (Was this bread bought yesterday?)

Read and answer

Before the students read the passage, ask them to look at the pictures and the title of the lesson and to guess what the patterns are or to say what they already know about them. Students then read the three questions and the passage and discuss the answers to the questions in pairs. Ask them to discuss the meaning of any unknown vocabulary and to look up words in their dictionaries if necessary. Check the answers with the class and answer any vocabulary questions. Then ask the students to pick out the examples of the passive which occur in the passage.

Finish off with a brief discussion on the content of the passage and ask the students why they think the lines were made and what they were used for.

Exercise 1

Refer students to the Look! box to remind them how to form the past passive. Students then do the exercise.

MODEL SUMMARY

The Nazca lines were made some time between 300 BC and AD 900. They were first discovered in the middle of this century. They can only be seen from the air, not the ground. Some people think that they were prehistoric 'computers' which were used to work out mathematical problems and to study the stars and some people think that they were runways for alien visitors from outer space.

Exercise 2

Before students start this activity, ask them to imagine what it was like to be one of the pilots who first saw the Nazca lines. Encourage them to discuss how the pilots must have felt. In pairs, students do the exercise, write the complete conversation in their notebooks and practise reading it. Then ask the students to act out the conversation without their notebooks and to try and sound excited. It is not important for them to reproduce the exact words they wrote down. Point out that *Over* is used in a conversation on a two-way radio to indicate that you have finished speaking and expect a reply and *Come in* is used to tell the pilots that they can start speaking to the control tower. *Well you'd better report back to base* means that the pilots had better return to their base.

Exercise 3

Do the exercise with the whole class first, eliciting the questions and answers from the students. Then students do it in pairs. Explain any unknown vocabulary, e.g: *to launch*. Point out that when we ask a question with *who* in the passive, we must say *by* at the end, e.g:

A: When was the telephone invented?
B: In 1876.
A: Who was it invented by?
B: Alexander Graham Bell.

Exercise 4

Practise a few questions with the whole class. Then, in pairs, students take it in turns to ask the question. Point out that *Did you know . . . ?* is the question and that it is followed by the affirmative form. So we say: *Did you know that the telephone was invented . . . ?* Finally, students write a sentence about each event.

 Oral exercises 4 and 5

Extra activities

1. Team Quiz

In teams, students write and then ask questions in the passive about historical events. The opposing team must answer, and then ask a question of their own. Award two points for each factually correct answer and take a point off any team which makes a grammatical mistake in a question or an answer.

2. Project Book

Ask the students to copy some of the patterns from the Students' Book into their project books and to write about what they think each one represents.

Activity Book Key

Exercise 1

1. It was knocked over and broken.
2. He was sent to his room.
3. It was damaged.
4. They were sent to bed.
5. It was (all) spilt on the carpet.
6. He was sent to his grandparents' house.

Exercise 2

1. When was Australia discovered?
   It was discovered in 1616.
2. When was radio invented?
   It was invented in 1895.
3. When was the White House built?
   It was built in 1792.
4. When was the typewriter invented?
   It was invented in 1829.
5. When were the mountains on the moon discovered?
   They were discovered in 1609.
6. When was the Eiffel Tower built?
   It was built in 1889.

Exercise 3

1. popular 2. astonishing 3. huge 4. pattern
5. mysterious 6. shapes 7. surface 8. visible
9. accurate 10. desert

Vocabulary	archaeologist	consist of
	coast guard	scuba dive
	expert	sink
	government	worth
	press	startling
	conference	officially
	reward	
	treasure	
	wreck	
Speechwork	Pronunciation: /eə/ fair, /ɪə/ fear	
	Stress: didadidi dadi, It MIGHT be a PRESent	
	Intonation: I'm 'sorry I didn't come,/but I forgot.	

Materials

Large pictures of people, e.g. from magazine advertisements.

Read and complete

Ask the students to look at the newspaper headline and the picture and to say what they think the article will be about. Explain *startling*. Students read the passage and find out if their predictions were correct. Tell them not to convert the verbs into the passive at this stage. After the first reading, write the unknown vocabulary on the board, e.g: *measure, worth*, etc.

Students find the vocabulary in the article and discuss what they think the meanings are in pairs. Check the students' understanding and clarify meaning. Tell the students that *sink* is an irregular verb and give them the three forms: *sink, sank, sunk*. The students then copy the article into their notebooks, writing the verbs in the past passive.

Before the students write the conversation between the journalist and John, elicit from the class the questions that the journalist is likely to ask.

Roleplay

Elicit an example conversation from the class. Put the students into pairs to roleplay the conversation. They then write it in their notebooks. Point out that *tea* in this conversation is likely to mean a cup of tea and something to eat, e.g. sandwiches and biscuits.

🔊 Listen

Ask students to read the task and to predict in pairs or small groups what the answers will be. Students then listen to the tape and find out if they were right. Check through the answers and play the tape again if necessary.

TAPESCRIPT
Listen to the next part of the Sherlock Holmes story, 'The Golden Glasses'.

Sherlock Holmes thinks the person who murdered Mr Smith must be the woman with the golden glasses. Holmes goes to the house and finds a mark on a cupboard door in the room where Mr Smith was murdered. He decides to talk to the cook, Mrs Marker, about it. Look at your book. Listen and choose the correct answers.

NARRATOR:
Sherlock Holmes looked at the door of the cupboard. Then he stood up and said: 'Look, there's a small mark on the lock by the keyhole. It is very new. Is the cook, Mrs Marker, here?'

'Yes,' said Detective Hopkins, 'Here she is.'

Holmes asked Mrs Marker: 'Did you see this mark when you cleaned the room yesterday?'

'No, I didn't.'

'I'm sure you didn't,' said Holmes. 'I think the person who killed Mr Smith made it.'

Holmes told Mrs Marker she could go. Then he said: 'Now I know what happened. The lady with the glasses came into this room. She went to the cupboard and tried to open it. Mr Smith came in while she was doing that. She quickly tried to take the key out of the lock. However, because she was in a hurry, she made a small mark as she was taking the key out. Smith went towards her and she picked up a knife and stabbed him. He fell on to the floor and she ran out of the room. But – she had lost her glasses!'

KEY
1. b 2. c 3. a

Write

Elicit suggestions for the first two sentences from the whole class. The present perfect is likely to be the most appropriate tense for these sentences so you may need to remind students of its use.

MODEL LETTER
Dear Jason,

I'm sorry I haven't written earlier. I've been very busy with exams but they've finished now. The school holidays have started, and I'd like to come and visit you soon if that's all right. I think I might be able to come in the first week of August but you'd better not plan anything special yet because I'm not sure. Please write soon.

Best wishes,
Jim

Dictionary skills

KEY: 1. headache 2. heading 3. headline
4. headquarters

Game

Examples are: *hole, lose, shoe, cross, sock, more, come, some, chess, her, lock, choose, close, cool.*

Grammar summary

Remind students that:

- *You'd better* is short for *You had better*
- *You'd better* is followed by the infinitive without *to*
- *This is(n't) the first/second time . . .* is followed by the present perfect
- *It can't/might/could/must be* is used to make deductions about the present when we have some information but we do not know the answer for sure
- the past passive is formed with *was/were* + past participle.

Extra Activities

1. Who is it?

Put some pictures of people on the board and number each picture. Give an oral description of each person in random order and, as you build up the description, ask the students to say which person they think you are describing. Prompt them into using *It might/could/must/can't be number . . . because . . .*

2. Jumbled sentences

Put the students into teams. Each team writes ten sentences using the structures in the grammar summary. They then cut each sentence into three pieces at any point (as long as they do not cut into a word), and pass all their pieces of paper in jumbled order to another team. The first team to re-order all their sentences correctly is the winner.

Activity Book Key

Exercise 1

1. I'm sorry I didn't feed the cats.
   I couldn't find the cat food.
   You'd better give them something to eat now.
2. I'm sorry my parents didn't come to the parent's meeting.
   I forgot to tell them about it.
   You'd better tell them about it next time.
3. I'm sorry I lost John's compass.
   It fell out of my pocket.
   You'd better buy him another one.
4. I'm sorry I haven't got the money.
   I left it in my purse at home.
   You'd better not forget it tomorrow.
5. I'm sorry I didn't get to the football match on time.
   I overslept, and missed the train.
   You'd better not be late next Saturday.
6. I'm sorry the radio isn't working.
   I forgot to buy some batteries.
   You'd better go and get some now.

Exercise 2

Numbers 1 to 3 are open.
4. Animal A is a mouse.
   Animal B is a cat.
   Animal C is a rabbit.
   Animal D is a seal.

Exercise 3

Two men were taken to the police station. The first man was given a cup of tea. He was asked about the accident but he didn't know anything. Then both men were driven back to the place where the accident happened. They were shown their cars. The first man's car was damaged but the other car was OK.

Exercise 4

1. c 2. b 3. b 4. a 5. b 6. a

Exercise 5

Open exercise

Exercise 6

1. could 2. can't 3. might 4. must 5. can't 6. must

Exercise 7

1. Yes, it was built in 1960.
2. Yes, it was opened by the Queen.
3. Yes, it was built in 1970.
4. Yes, it was opened a year later.
5. Yes, some old jewellery was found.
6. Yes, it was given to a museum.

Speechwork Lessons 41–45

Pronunciation

Listen and repeat.
/eə/ /eə/ /eə/ fair pear hair

Listen and repeat.
/ɪə/ /ɪə/ /ɪə/ fear pier here

Listen and repeat.
Which is Mary?
She's over there.
She's got fair hair.
She's eating a pear.
Great! She's here.

Stress

Listen and repeat.
didadidi dadi, didadidi dadi, didadidi dadi
It MIGHT be a PRESent,
It COULD be a RECord,
It MUST be a SWEATer

Intonation

Listen and repeat.
I'm 'sorry I didn't come, but I forgot.
I'm 'sorry I didn't phone, but I was late.
I'm 'sorry I didn't go, but I was busy.

I wish he didn't.

Language use	Make wishes about things that are not true
Grammar	Verb *wish* + past tense: *I wish I was tall* (but I'm not.) *I wish I didn't have* a baby brother (but I do.) *I wish I could* waterski (but I can't.) *I wish I lived* in London (but I don't.)
Vocabulary	birthmark Worse luck! avoid go out with somebody take notice wish

Background notes
genie (AB) A magical spirit in Arabian fairy stories.

Presentation
Establish a situation to introduce the structure. Tell the students about Judy and her sister Penny. Judy lives in the city and works in an office. Penny lives in the countryside and works on a farm. They often visit each other and each of them thinks that her sister has a better life than she does. They are talking to each other.

Introduce *wish*. Say: *Judy is thinking about the countryside. She would like to live in the countryside. She says to her sister, 'I wish I lived in the countryside.'*

Point out that Judy is wishing for something that is not likely to happen. Highlight the grammatical form: *wish* + past simple, but explain that it is used to talk about your wishes in the *present*. Elicit more sentences arising from the situation and drill each sentence chorally and individually, e.g:

JUDY: I wish I didn't live in the city. I wish I worked on a farm.

PENNY: I wish I didn't live in the countryside. I wish I was an office worker.

Note: *Wish* is followed by the past subjunctive. This has the same form as the past simple so it is probably less complicated to tell students to use the past simple. The only difference is that strictly speaking the past subjunctive of the verb *to be* is *were* for all persons. However, *I wish I was* is now quite commonly used.

Dialogue and Exercise 1
Ask the students to look at the picture. Write a focus question on the board: *What does Kate think of the boy?* Play the tape. The students listen with books closed and answer the focus question.

The students then read the questions in Exercise 1. Explain *avoid*. Students listen again and answer the questions. They then read the dialogue. Explain any new vocabulary, e.g: *to annoy, to go out with*, etc.

Point out that *Timbuktu* is used to represent a place which is very far away. The students listen to the paused version and repeat.

Exercise 2
Point out that *es* is added to *wish* in the third person singular. Explain *birthmark* and any other unknown vocabulary.

Exercise 3
Refer students to the Look! box and elicit a few example sentences about what the students wish. They then think about their wishes and tell their partner in pairs. Ask them to use the questionnaire as a guideline.

Exercise 4
MODEL DIALOGUE

FATHER: What's the matter?

YOU: Oh, I've got too much homework to do each night. I wish I had more free time.

FATHER: Well, you have to do homework if you go to school.

YOU: I wish I didn't have to go to school.

FATHER: But everyone has to go to school.

YOU: Well, I wish they didn't have to. I'd rather stay at home.

 Oral exercises 1 and 2

Extra activities

1. Your dream town
Put the students into groups to exchange ideas about what they would like to change and what new things they would like to have in their town. Encourage them to use *wish*, e.g: *I/We wish there was a swimming pool.* Then ask the students to make a list of the ideas and to put them into order of priority. The groups can compare and discuss their priorities at the end.

2. Discussion
Follow up the topic of the dialogue with a discussion. Write some questions on the board: *Are you ever followed by boys/girls? Does it annoy you? Do you ever follow boys/girls? Do boys/girls sometimes stare at you? Does it annoy you? Do you stare at boys/girls?*

In groups, students compare and discuss their experiences. If you have a mixed sex class, put them into single-sex groups. The groups should then report back to each other. Encourage them to discuss the different behaviour and experiences of boys and girls and what they think the reasons are for this.

Activity Book Key

Exercise 1
1. I wish I understood the question.
2. I wish I could write quickly.
3. I wish I knew the answers.
4. I wish I had a calculator.
5. I wish my pen was working properly.

Exercise 2
1. wishing well 2. wedding cake 3. shooting star
4. wishbone 5. lamp

Exercise 3
Open exercise

Exercise 4
Open exercise

LESSON 47 # If I were you . . .

Language use	Give advice
Grammar	Second conditional: *If* + clause in past simple (past subjunctive) + clause with *would* + infinitive: *If I were* you, *I'd tell* your mother. *If you had* a new hobby, *you wouldn't be* so bored.
Vocabulary	martial arts lonely fed up miserable fun Never mind!

Background notes
Chris A boy's or girl's name. It is usually short for *Christopher* (boy's name) or *Christine* (girl's name).

Presentation
Tell the students that a friend of theirs has just won £2,000 (or the equivalent in their currency) in a competition. The friend cannot decide what to do with the money and the students are talking to her/him and giving advice. Ask the students for ideas on how the friend should spend £2,000, e.g: go on a holiday, buy some clothes and records, give some of the money to charity, etc. Elicit a few ideas from the class, then each student notes down how they think the money should be spent. They may decide on one thing or on a number of things. Give them a little time to think about it, then ask for their suggestions and lead into a presentation of *If I were you . . .*, e.g:
T: What have you written down?
S: A holiday in the United States.
T: You can say to your friend: 'If I were you, I'd have a holiday in the United States.'

Point out, in the L1 if necessary, that:
● this structure is the second conditional
● it is used to describe an imaginary or hypothetical situation. I am imagining being you and having £1,000 to spend and so I say, *If I were you . . .* It is therefore used here to give advice
● it refers to the present or future. *. . . I'd go to the United States*, i.e. now or in the future
● we can say *If I were you . . .* or *If I was you . . .*
● the main clause uses *would* + infinitive (without *to*)
● *would* is often contracted to *'d*, e.g. *I'd buy . . .*
● the *if* clause can come first or second.
Go on to elicit and practice other example sentences.

Text
Ask the students to cover up the problem letter on the page and just to read the answer. Explain *lonely*. Then discuss in pairs and then as a class what they think the first letter said. They read the first letter and find out if they were right. Check their understanding by asking them to tell you what Chris's problem is and what advice is given. See if the students can deduce the meaning of *fed up* and explain it if necessary.
    Students then underline the examples of the second conditional in the answer. Point out that the second conditional doesn't always start with *If I were you . . .* Any verb can be used in the *if* clause. The verb in the *if* clause should be in the past simple form. Students copy the examples of the second conditional into their notebooks.

Exercise 1
Elicit Chris's first two lines from the class and drill lines 1 to 4 of the conversation. Then put the students into pairs to complete it.

Exercise 3
Students read the situations. Explain *to take up* (martial arts) and any other unknown vocabulary. Elicit advice for each situation from the class. Give the students any vocabulary they need. Do an example with the class first, e.g:
s: I've lost my watch and it was really expensive.
т: Oh no! Well, if I were you, I'd go to lost property.
Students practise in pairs.

 Exercise 5
Students read the task and listen to the tape. In pairs, they discuss and compare their answers. Check the answers with the class. Then write on the board the following phrasal verbs and expressions from the tape: *on the line, I've been going steady with him, hang on, very keen on you, you're going off to, settle down, straight out, get on with your studies, I'll have a try*. Play the tape again, stop it at these words/ expressions and ask students to try to guess their meaning. Discuss the meanings with the class.

TAPESCRIPT
Listen to this caller on the radio phone-in programme and take notes.

WOMAN: And now for our next caller. I think we've got Ann on the line? Hello? Ann? Are you there?
ANN: Yes. Hello. Um, well it's about my boyfriend. I've been going steady with him for just over two years but you see I'm leaving to go to college next year and he wants to come with me and I don't think . . .
WOMAN: Hang on. Let me see if I've understood you right. You've got a boyfriend who's very keen on you, right?
ANN: Right.
WOMAN: And you're going off to college next year?
ANN: Yes. In September.
WOMAN: And this is in another part of the country, is it?
ANN: Yes. I live in Essex and I'm going to college in Northampton. And now he wants to move to Northampton and try and get a job there so he can be with me.
WOMAN: And you don't want that?
ANN: Well . . . No. I mean, I'm not sure. I don't think I want to settle down yet.
WOMAN: Well, Ann, I think you ought to tell your boyfriend straight out that you don't want him to move to Northampton with you. You want to get on with your studies and that you think it's a good idea to be away from each other for a while. This way you'll both know if you really love one another. How does that sound to you? Do you think your boyfriend would accept that?
ANN: Mmm. Maybe. I'll have a try, anyway.
WOMAN: Good. Well, the best of luck, Ann. And now we have Harry on the line . . .

Exercise 6
Elicit an example letter from the class. Check that the students understand that they must use *would* because the conditional clause *if I met . . .* is understood, even though it is not stated. Point out that it is not necessary to repeat *would* in a list of two or more activities, e.g: *We would drink champagne and eat caviar.* The students should then each write a letter on their own.

 Oral exercise 3

Extra activities

1. Team game
Write some prompt words on the board, e.g: *shoes, English, money, homework, hungry, headache, toothache, tired.* Put the students into teams. Team A uses one of the words on the board to explain a problem and Team B replies by giving advice using *If I were you . . .* If the sentence of advice is correct and logical, Team B is given a point. Team B then explains a problem to Team A and a student from Team A gives advice, etc. e.g:
A: My shoes have broken. I only bought them last week.
B: If I were you, I'd take them back to the shop.
B: I find English really difficult.
A: If I were you, I'd study French.

2. Find a problem page
Ask the students to find a problem page in a newspaper or magazine (in their own language). They then choose one of the letters and replies, and write an approximate translation in English, at home.

Activity Book Key

Exercise 1
1. T 2. F 3. T 4. T 5. F

Exercise 2
1. If I were you, I'd give up smoking.
2. If I were you, I'd write to your parents.
3. If I were you, I'd take more exercise.
4. If I were you, I'd eat proper food.
5. If I were you, I'd get up earlier.
6. If I were you, I'd watch less TV.

Exercise 3
1. If he gave up smoking, he'd have more money.
2. If he wrote to his parents, he'd feel less homesick.
3. If he took more exercise, he'd feel more healthy.
4. If he ate proper food, he wouldn't feel so hungry.
5. If he got up earlier, he'd have more time.
6. If he watched less TV, he'd have fewer headaches.

Language use	Comprehension, summary and vocabulary skills	
Vocabulary	fear	push
	feather	remind
	goose	gentle
	hunchback	romantic
	lighthouse	rough
	mouth (of river)	

Background notes

Literary extract The extract is from *The Snow Goose*, included in the selection *The Snow Goose and Other Short Stories* by Paul Gallico, New Method Supplementary Readers Stage 3. The stories are all about courage and faith in adversity.

Read and listen and Exercise 1

Pre-teach *lighthouse, hunchback* and *snow goose*. Students read and listen to the text and discuss the answers to the questions in Exercise 1 in pairs. They then read the story again. Check the answers to Exercise 1 with the class and answer any vocabulary questions.

Write the following words on the board as prompts and elicit an oral summary of the story from the class: *Philip Rhayader, hunchback, lighthouse, birds, One afternoon a girl . . ., large white bird, afraid, snow goose.*

Exercise 3

MODEL DIALOGUE

GIRL: Hello, Mum. I'm sorry I'm late for lunch.
MOTHER: Where have you been?
GIRL: To the lighthouse. I went to see the hunchback.
MOTHER: The hunchback! Why?
GIRL: Because I found a large white bird and it was hurt. I wanted the hunchback to make it better.
MOTHER: What sort of bird was it?
GIRL: He said it was a snow goose.

Joke time!

Check that the students understand that *make someone sick* has a literal meaning and an idiomatic meaning. The sea can make you sick, i.e. cause you to feel sick, and a person can make you sick, i.e. annoy/irritate you.

Extra activities

1. Philip's diary

Ask the students to imagine they are Philip Rhayader and to write his diary for the day the girl came to see him.

2. Finish the story

Put the students into groups to predict what happens next, in the story of the snow goose. Ask them to work out an ending to the story. A representative from each group should then tell the group's story to the rest of the class.

Activity Book Key

Exercise 1

1. /guːs/   2. noun   3. gander   4. geese   5. /giːs/
6. large   7. white   8. duck   9. hissing noise
10. gosling

Exercise 2

TAPESCRIPT

Look at your book. Listen to the commentary about sea diving and write the answers to the questions.

ANDREA: Philip and I continued our explorations off the coast of Florida. We didn't have much luck, until one day when we made a very strange discovery. I had just finished a two-hour dive, and Philip was down below. He sent me a message which sounded very exciting.
PHILIP: Andrea, I think I've found something.
ANDREA: What can you see, Phil?
PHILIP: It's an enormous object. It's a bit difficult to see down here, but it looks like a ship.
ANDREA: Can you get any closer to it?
PHILIP: Not really, it's on the edge of a cliff and it might move.
ANDREA: It's on the edge of a cliff?
PHILIP: Yes, and it's so dark down here I can't see. The water's too dark. I'll come up to the surface. We'll get the lights and start tomorrow.
ANDREA: We didn't know it at the time, but we had found a four-hundred-year-old ship full of historical treasures. Our voyage into the past was about to begin.

KEY
1. They are Philip and Andrea.
2. Philip was making the dive.
3. It looks like a ship.
4. Because it's on the edge of a cliff.
5. Because it's so dark.
6. It's a four-hundred-year-old ship.

Exercise 3
Open exercise

Exercise 4

goose	geese	wolf	wolves
luggage	U	sheep	sheep
theory	theories	chess	U
mouse	mice	ice-lolly	ice-lollies
information	U	deer	deer

My favourite magazine

Language use	Make suggestions
	Make generalisations about groups of people
Grammar	Modal verbs *could, should, ought to:*
	We could have a fashion page.
	I think we should have a competition
	We ought to have a sports page.
	Adjectives *not many, all:*
	Not many people like cookery.
	We all like the problem letters.
	Pronouns *nobody, something, anything:*
	Nobody likes the career guide.
Vocabulary	advice gossip
	career hairdo
	cartoon make-up
	competition model
	cookery review
	editor tip
	fashion fabulous
	feature sensational
	free offer

Materials
Photostories

Introduction
Introduce the theme of magazines and pre-teach some vocabulary. Give the students a minute to write down the names of all the teenage magazines they can think of and ask the student with the longest list to read it out. Ask the students what kinds of things are included in the magazines and, as they tell you, teach them the vocabulary they need to describe these things, e.g: *photostory, fashion, reviews, special features, regular features*, etc.

Read and answer
Give the students one minute to read, then ask them to name five features in 'Streetbeat' without looking at their books. The students then look at their books again, listen to the radio commercial for 'Streetbeat' and tell you what is good about the magazine. Answer any questions on vocabulary.

Exercise 1
Check that the students understand all the vocabulary in the exercise. Ask them to do it alone and then to compare their lists in pairs. If you have a mixed-sex class, the students could be put into pairs of one boy and girl (or threes if the numbers are not equal) and the class could discuss the difference between boys' and girls' favourite magazine features.

Presentation and Exercise 3
Tell the students that they are going to produce a class magazine and they must decide on eight features to include in the magazine. Ask them for ideas. As they offer ideas, revise the language of suggestion, *How/What about* + noun/gerund e.g: *What about including a penpal column?* and *Let's . . .,* e.g: *Let's have a pop music competition.* Lead into an introduction of *We could/should/ought to have . . .* Point out that:
- *we could . . .* is another way of making a suggestion
- *we should . . .* and *we ought to . . .* are strong suggestions. *We should have a pop gossip page* means that you think it is very important to have a pop gossip page
- *ought to* is like *should*
- *could* and *should* are followed by the infinitive without *to. Ought* is followed by the infinitive with *to*
- the negative is formed by putting *not* after *could, should* and *ought*.

Elicit or provide a model sentence for each modal verb and drill it. Ask students to study the example in the Look! box. They then carry out the instructions in Exercise 3.

Exercise 4
Introduce the tape with a brief discussion about photostories.

Students then look at the task in their books. Play the tape. Pause it two or three times to give students the time to take notes. As you do so, explain any vocabulary that students need in order to do the task, e.g: *shy, rarely, recently, reasonably attractive, deformity, ordinary, the lines, recite the alphabet.* Students compare their notes in pairs. Play the tape again so that they can check their answers.

Go through the task with the class and encourage them to discuss their reactions to what David said. If students find it very difficult, divide the listening into short sections corresponding to the three questions in the task. Get the students to guess the answer that David will give. Guide them into doing this, e.g. Say: *David says boys and girls are different. How? Listen.*

TAPESCRIPT
Listen to David talking about his work for a teenage magazine. He takes photographs for photostories. Look at your book and take notes.

INTERVIEWER:	Do you use professional models and actors and actresses or do you just use people that you know?
DAVID:	We very rarely use . . . er . . . models or actors or actresses. Usually use people that are just . . . er . . . known to us, or known to our friends, but there's quite often a

problem with the men or the boys 'cos the boys are very shy, so we quite often have to get models for the male parts.

INTERVIEWER: So you have a sort of idea if you want a fair-haired girl or a dark-haired girl, if you want somebody tall or somebody short.

DAVID: They're not usually specified, unless it's specifically about their appearance, then it's really up to me which . . . er . . . girl it is. It doesn't have to be blonde or brunette so long as they're reasonably attractive; but on the other hand they could be quite ordinary. They don't have to be model-like. When they are model-like, it tends to look a bit false.

INTERVIEWER: When you've got your models and you've decided on the day when you're going to do the photography and you've arrived at the place where you're going to do it, how do you get the girls and the boys to do what you want for the picture?

DAVID: Well it's easy if they've done it before but not so easy if they haven't, and the boys are usually quite difficult. They tend to hang back and be very shy, especially if there's more than one boy, they tend to go and stand in the corner and look a bit . . . er . . . out of it all. Basically we try to do it like a moving film so that we . . . er . . . shoot a lot and keep telling them to do things all the time – talking to them, shouting at them if necessary – and actually get them to speak the lines that in the end will be written on the page in bubbles; and if they can't do that because it's something silly and they feel really embarrassed about saying it, we just get them to recite the alphabet to each other. Anything so they look as if they're doing something, and it usually works in the end.

 Oral exercise 4

Extra activities

1. Photostories

Divide the students into groups and give each group a photostory cut up into individual pictures. They arrange the pictures in the correct order and then work out what each character is saying in English. They do not need to provide an exact translation of what is written in their language. (If the story is easy to work out from the pictures, you could provide blank speech bubbles for the students to write in.) The groups then act out their stories to each other.

2. Comparing magazines

Ask the students to bring in copies of some teenage magazines and some adult magazines. The students then compare them and discuss the differences. Write a list of things to be compared on the board to guide their discussion, e.g: *contents page, stories, advertisements, problem page, fashion, feature articles, pictures, price.* The discussion should incorporate the use of *more, less, fewer* and comparative adjectives and adverbs, e.g: *There are fewer pictures in the adult magazines. The teenage magazines are more brightly-coloured.*

Activity Book Key

Exercise 1

1. F 2. F 3. T 4. T 5. T 6. F 7. F 8. T

Exercise 2
Open exercise

Exercise 3
Yes, I think we should.
Yes, I think we ought to.
Yes, I think we could.
Yes, I think we ought to.
Yes, I think we could.
Yes, I think we ought to.

Vocabulary	barometer
	cot
	customer
	size
	tractor
	existing
Speechwork	Pronunciation: /eə/ fairy,
	/e/ ferry
	Stress: dida dida dida,
	You OUGHT to JOIN a CLUB.
	Intonation: If 'I were you,/I'd
	'tell your mother.

Discussion

Put the students into groups for the discussion. If they do not have many ideas about what to do and see, write a few on the board to help them, e.g: *The Tower of London, Buckingham Palace, the Houses of Parliament, the British Museum, Oxford, Cambridge, the mountains of Scotland, a play at Stratford-upon-Avon, Brighton, a rock concert, the London underground, Hampton Court, Windsor Castle, Windsor Safari Park, Madame Tussaud's, Oxford Street.* If there is a British Tourist Authority office in your town, you could ask them for some leaflets which the students could consult in their discussion.

Write

Elicit a model letter from the class, then ask the students to write their own letters individually.

MODEL LETTER

Dear Mr and Mrs Phillips,

I am writing to tell you a few things about myself before I come to stay with you. My name is Luciano Borrello, I am sixteen and I come from Italy. In my spare time, I like reading magazines, listening to rock music and going to discos. While I'm in Britain, I'd like to go to London and see the Tower of London, Buckingham Palace and the Houses of Parliament and travel on the London underground. I'd also like to visit Oxford and Cambridge and see the old college buildings. And of course I'd like to practise my English as much as possible. Oh, I think you should know that I don't like fish. I hope that's all right.

I'm looking forward to meeting you.

Yours sincerely,

Luciano Borrello

Discuss and write

Students decide what time of year they are going to visit Britain and think about what to take. They should remember that it rains a lot in Britain and the weather changes very often. Before the students start working in pairs, remind them of the structure: *I think we should/ought to (take a . . .).*

When the students have written and compared their lists, you could tell them that they can only take a small bag with them and they must reduce their list to a specified number of items, e.g. seven. Put them into small groups to discuss and reach an agreement on a new reduced list.

Listen and discuss

Ask the students to read the introduction and instructions. Put students into groups and play the tape once. Students discuss the possibilities. If necessary, play the tape again. Ask the students to plan their weekend in London using the ideas on 'London Information Line' and any other ideas of their own.

TAPESCRIPT

You are now in Britain. It is Saturday morning and you are not sure what to do at the weekend. Listen to the telephone recording of 'London Information Line'. Make notes of some of the things you can do, and in groups, discuss which sounds the most interesting or exciting.

ANNOUNCER:

Welcome to 'London Information Line' – a guide to activities and events in London this Saturday.

For those of you who like plenty of action, there's the Wind and Surf Show at Alexandra Palace in Wood Green, North London. There you can see and try all the latest windsurfing and surfing equipment. It's open from ten in the morning until seven in the evening.

Still with action in mind, if you don't mind a day outside, there's a special BMX bike rally at Romford starting at 11 o'clock. All the BMX stars from Europe and the US will be there.

In a quieter mood, for music lovers there's currently a series of music films at the British Library. These are in the Seminar Room and tickets are available at the main door. Today's film is about the life of the British composer Benjamin Britten and starts at 2.30 pm.

For theatre lovers there's a treat in store at the Olivier Theatre on the South Bank, where the National Theatre Company are presenting a new production of Bertolt Brecht's 'Threepenny Opera', starring Tim Curry. This is a colourful tale of life in Berlin between the wars and it starts at 7 pm.

And if none of these interest you, why not take a river trip up the Thames from Westminster Bridge to Hampton Court, the beautiful palace which once belonged to Henry VIII? If you time your trip well, you can see the Son et Lumière, starting at 8 pm, and still get the boat back to London.

Write

Elicit a model postcard from the class. Each student then writes her/his own postcard.

MODEL POSTCARD

Dear Mum and Dad,

I'm having a fantastic time! The weather is quite good. It has only rained once. The food is not as good as French food but I like the fish and chips. We've been to London twice. We went to Madame Tussaud's the first time and then went shopping in Oxford Street last time. I bought you a present there. Yesterday we went to Cambridge and saw the old colleges. They're really beautiful.

See you soon.

Love,

Marie-Pierre

Discuss

Elicit a few suggestions for presents from the whole class first. Ask them to look at the pictures if they have not got any ideas about what to buy. Put them into pairs for the discussion and remind them to use *If I were you, . . .* and *You could/should/ought to buy . . .*

MODEL DISCUSSION

S1: If I were you, I'd buy your parents some English tea.

S2: They don't really like tea.

S1: Well, you could buy them some marmalade then. English marmalade and Scottish marmalade are very good.

S2: Yes, that's a good idea. And what about my friend Emma?

S1: Well, if I were you, I'd buy her a T-shirt with something about London on it.

Roleplay

Tell the students that they want to buy a T-shirt. Build up an example dialogue with the help of the class. Remind students how to form a relative clause. They may need to use a relative clause in the *Have you got a/any . . . ?* question. Put the students into pairs to take it in turns to play the customer and the shop assistant. The students should buy the presents which they decided to get in the discussion.

MODEL ROLEPLAY

A: Can I help you?

B: Yes, I'd like a T-shirt. Have you got any T-shirts which say 'I love London'?

A: Yes. What size do you want?

B: Medium, please. How much is it?

A: It's £4.

B: I think I'll take it, please.

Dictionary skills

ACROSS 2. barometer 3. cot

DOWN 1. tractor

Grammar summary

Remind students that:

- *wish* is followed by the past tense when talking about your wishes for the present and/or the future
- the second conditional is formed with *if* + past tense, *would* + infinitive without *to*. It refers to now or the future and is often used to give advice.

 Oral exercise 5

Extra activities

1. Team Quiz

Put the students into teams and ask them to prepare quiz questions for each other about the Students' Book. You could allocate half of the book to each team and ask them to plan their questions using those lessons. If you think they will find this difficult, you could ask them the questions. Inform students the day before that the quiz will take place and ask them to look through their books.

EXAMPLE QUESTIONS

Where does Andy Morgan live? (Dover.)

What's the name of the company Rick Hunter works for? (Anything Is Possible)

Who went around the world in eighty days? (Phileas Fogg.)

Who discovered the hot-air balloon? (The Montgolfier brothers.)

What member of the Royal Family did Kate and Andy see? (Princess Diana.)

What was the statue of the Happy Prince doing when the swallow saw it? (Crying.)

Who was a queen for only nine days and was beheaded in the Tower of London? (Lady Jane Grey.)

Where can you see killer whale, dolphin and sea lion shows? (Windsor Safari Park.)

2. Information Line

Ask the students to produce an information line about their town (or a nearby town or city) like the 'London Information Line'. They will need to find out what events are taking place in the town. Ask them to discuss what they need to do and to divide up the research work between them. When they have written the information line, make a recording of some of them reading it.

Activity Book Key

Exercise 1

1. I wish I was tall.
2. I wish I had some money.
3. I wish I had a lot of friends.
4. I wish I didn't feel ill.
5. I wish I was good at sport.
6. I wish I didn't have a headache.

Exercise 2
Numbers 3 and 4 are correct.

CORRECTED SENTENCES
1. If you joined a club, you'd make some new friends.
2. You'd feel better if you went to bed.
5. If I left home, I would go and live with my sister.
6. I'd go and see him if I were you.

Exercise 3

FASHION	PENFRIEND
CHEMIST	PUZZLE
SENSATIONAL	ASLEEP
GENTLE	FEATHER

Exercise 4
ought, thought, bought, fought, caught, taught, rough, enough, tough, stuff

Exercise 5
1. fed up 2. visible 3. avoid 4. trumpet 5. explore 6. forecast

Exercise 6
Open exercise

Exercise 7
Open exercise

Activity Book Key Final Roundup

1 C	A	2 P	T	3 U	R	4 E			5 R		6 S	O	F	7 T
L		R		S		8 A	9 S	L	E	E	P			R
10 O	M	E	L	E	T	T	E		L		11 O	N	T	O
A		H		D			A		I		O			P
K		12 I	N	T	E	13 L	L	14 I	G	15 E	N	T		I
R		S		O		O		16 T	I	N				C
17 O	U	T				V			18 O	D	19 D			A
O		O			20 P	E	21 T		U		22 R	E	A	L
23 M	A	R	V	E	L	L	O	24 U	S		A			
		I			25 E	Y	E	S		26 T	W	I	N	27 S
28 L	U	C	K		A				29 T					T
O					S		30 A		31 A	R	32 M			A
33 S	U	N	G	L	A	S	S	E	S		34 E	A	S	T
E					N				T					U
35 R	O	M	A	N	T	I	C		36 E	S	C	A	P	E

Speechwork Lessons 46–50

Pronunciation
Listen and repeat.
/eə/ /eə/ /eə/ fairy vary Mary
/e/ /e/ /e/ ferry very merry

Listen and repeat.
Did you see Mary?
Yes, she was on the ferry.
She was very merry.

Stress
Listen and repeat.
dida dida dida, dida dida dida, dida dida dida
You OUGHT to JOIN a CLUB,
You OUGHT to TALK to JOHN,
They OUGHT to TELL their FRIENDS

Intonation
Listen and repeat.
If 'I were you,/I'd 'tell your mother.
If 'I were you,/I'd 'stay in bed.
If 'I were you,/I'd 'take an aspirin.

Grammatical item	Example sentences	Lesson number

Verbs: main tenses

1. Present simple — *Andy Morgan lives in Dover.* — 1

2. Present continuous
future use — *He is taking his 'O' level examinations in two years' time.* — 1

3. Simple future
(See also Modals) — *Will it hurt?* — 21
The injection won't hurt.

4. Past simple — *When did you go?* — 3
I went last summer.
When I reached the graveyard, I began to feel afraid. — 38

5. Present perfect simple
experience — *Have you ever been to Britain?* — 3
Yes, I have.
I've been to Britain twice.

with *how long, for* and *since* — *How long have you hitch-hiked?* — 4
I've hitch-hiked since I was 16/for two years.

with *yet, just* and *already* — *He hasn't started it yet.* — 6
He's just started it.
I've already found a job.

with *first/second time* — *This is(n't) the first time he's been late.* — 41

6. Present perfect continuous
with *how long, for* and *since* — *How long have you been living here?* — 32
I've been living here since November/for three weeks.

7. Past continuous — *What were you doing there?* — 11
I was visiting relations.

in contrast with past simple — *She was opening a building when we saw her.* — 11
with *as* — *As I was walking through the rose garden, I saw a young woman.* — 12

with *while* — *While I was walking along, I saw someone in the rose garden.* — 12

8. Past perfect simple
in contrast with past simple — *When he got back, he discovered that someone had taken his suitcase.* — 37

Verbs: other forms

1. Modals
needn't (refusal of offers) — *You needn't bother.* — 2
will (promises) — *I'll send you a postcard.* — 2
(offers) — *I'll make some tea.* — 2
shall (offers) — *Shall I take your rucksack for you?* — 2
would rather (preference) — *I'd rather watch 'Miami Vice'.* — 18
may (speculation) — *It may hurt a little.* — 21
used to (past habits) — *I used to like swimming but I don't now.* — 22
must (strong advice) — *You must train more regularly.* — 28
(deduction) — *It must be the postman.* — 42
have got to (obligation) — *I've got to go on a survival course.* — 31
had better (advice) — *You'd better go without him.* — 41
(warning) — *You'd better not be late again.* — 41
can't (deduction) — *It can't be from Gran.* — 42
might (deduction) — *It might be from Cindy.* — 42
could (deduction) — *It could be chocolates.* — 42
(suggestions) — *We could have a fashion page.* — 49
should (suggestions) — *I think we should have a competition.* — 49
ought to (suggestions) — *We ought to have a sports page.* — 49

2. Gerunds
after *like/enjoy* — *I enjoy gliding.* — 9
as subject — *Gliding is much more fun than ballooning.* — 9
after *quite like/enjoy/don't like/prefer* — *I prefer watching sports programmes.* — 18

111

4. Contrast
   however

Dolphins in the wild usually live for more than 30 years. However, in captivity, most die before their twelfth birthday. — 19

Adverbial clauses

1. Condition
   if (first conditional)

If I hit the spaceship, I'll stop. — 26
If you don't look behind the satellite door, you won't find the sword. — 27,28

   (second conditional)

If I were you, I'd tell your mother. — 47
If you had a new hobby, you wouldn't be so bored.

2. Time
   until

Drive down the A20 until you reach the B2163. — 7

Relative clauses

1. Defining relative clauses
   with *who*
   with *which*

Andy is an English boy who lives in Dover. — 1,34
Alaska is a territory which is situated in North America. — 34

   with *where*

This is a video where the performers play and sing their song. — 39

2. Non-defining relative clauses
   with *where*

He goes to Castle Hill Secondary School, where he is in his third year. — 1

3. Contact clauses
   omitting *whom*

Someone (whom) he admires very much is Bob Geldof. — 1

   omitting *which*

The subjects (which) he likes best are Geography and Computer Studies. — 1

Reported speech

   with *say, know, hope* and *think*

He said (that) he couldn't continue. — 33
We knew (that) the end was near.

Prepositions

1. Direction and position
   at
   down
   into
   on
   above
   across

Turn off at Exit B. — 7
Drive down the A20. — 7
Turn left into Drayton Road. — 7
Take the next turning on the right. — 7
The aeroplane flew high above the clouds. — 34
You have to walk across the bridge to get to the other side. — 34

   along
   among

She walked carefully along the edge of the cliff. — 34
Among the pile of photographs, she found one of her mother. — 34

   around
   below
   over
   through

If you wrap this around your ankle, it'll feel better. — 34
The fish swam just below the surface of the water. — 34
We flew right over the Tower of London. — 34
He hurried through the dark forest. — 34

2. Miscellaneous
   of
   from

My table is made of wood. — 36
Butter is made from cream. — 36